# Spend, Protect, Grow

## A Comprehensive Guide to Maintaining Your Desired Lifestyle Throughout Retirement

Phil Simonides, CFP®
Executive Vice President
McAdam Financial

Phil Simonides, CFP®
Executive Vice President
McAdam Financial
8000 Towers Crescent Drive, 13th Floor
Vienna, VA 22182

Book layout ©2022 Advisors Excel, LLC

Spend, Protect, Grow/Phil Simonides

ISBN 9798344098999

*"If you don't have the time to do it right,
when will you have the time to do it over?*

*~ John Wooden*

*I'd like to dedicate this book to my late father and mother,
Constantine B. Simonides (1934-1994)
and Betty L. Simonides (1934-2018).*

*They made me.*

# Table of Contents

# The Importance of Planning

O f all the ways my team and I at McAdam Financial work with clients, the first and most prevalent is as educators. There is so much erroneous conventional wisdom and so-called "factual" information on the internet that our clients can unwittingly put themselves, their assets, and their entire wealth at risk.

We see it with almost every new client. However, we leverage our financial education and share it with them to *de-risk their retirement.*

The risks are many. One is the supposed "wisdom" out there, and our first job is to gently inform clients that much of it is just plain false. Instead, we give them options to replace it so that they may achieve better financial results — better *lifetime* results.

De-risking your retirement is what we do best. It is well and good to save lots of money while you earn it. Why give it away or lose it due to wrong information or lack of planning thereafter?

At McAdam, we are not just investment managers; we are comprehensive financial planners. We specialize in reducing and even eliminating the risks to your wealth so it is there for you throughout your retirement.

Just as in any other profession, financial advisors have different areas of focus and specialization. At McAdam, we combine three specific things when planning with our clients. We like to refer to them as our "three uniques." When we use all three of them together for you, they represent a powerful and holistic de-risking strategy for your investment assets and retirement.

## First Unique

We refer to the first unique as "Holistic Advisor." Usually, when people see or hear that word, they think of holistic medicine, but here, it has a slightly different meaning.

Being your "Holistic Advisor" is much more about comprehensive financial planning with you. For us, financial planning is about determining your goals and objectives upfront, examining all the resources you have to accomplish them, and then finding the best path to deploy those resources to help you reach and achieve all of your goals.

We consider everything we are looking at for a client simultaneously. Because we look at the whole picture at once, we follow what the CFP board says is the optimal method for comprehensive financial planning. We do charge a fee for financial planning, whereas many other firms do not.

It's important to note that there are really only three reasons why financial advisors don't charge a fee for financial planning:
1. They are not good at planning — and they know it — so they give it away for free.
2. They are not licensed to charge a planning fee, which is required to do so.
3. They (or their firm) do not care about planning because they are primarily financial salespeople or asset

gatherers and are not focused on their clients' goals, concerns, and objectives.

A second essential element of being holistic is that we are completely and totally independent at McAdam. We don't "make" anything like many other firms; we don't have in-house products that our advisors are required to "push." When other firms create their own financial products, there's pressure on their advisors to sell them before even looking at other options. We don't do that at McAdam. We have access to *all* products in the marketplace. We are continuously vetting products in pursuit of the optimal ones, and thus, we can help you choose what best suits your goals and needs.

## Second Unique

Our second unique area of expertise is "Safe Money Strategies" (SMS). This method of investing allows you to make an initial investment you are guaranteed never to lose while still having the opportunity to grow and profit. Every time that investment grows, the increased value establishes a new "floor" that it cannot go below — a sort of "profit and lock it in" or "ratcheting" effect that repeats over and over.

That pattern in this approach to investing is uniquely helpful in retirement for people who do not want to give back a single dollar of what they've already made. At many firms, they do not focus on this at all. At McAdam, it's one of our specialties.

## Third Unique

We refer to the third unique as "Process-Driven Portfolio Management." Many people in the money management industry use some sort of analytical process. Ours, however, is very specific and proprietary.

When we compare our process to what other companies do, there's at least one original step most of them don't take. That step helps drive the results we're looking to achieve for our clients. At McAdam, we named this approach "Strategic Diversification Services" (SDS).

If you try to find an advisor who combines all three unique approaches and toolkits, it will likely be less than 1 percent of all advisors in any given marketplace.

This combination of uniques is how McAdam advisors can create the complete set of written plans we'll discuss next. There are five plans, each with a distinct purpose. Certainly, not all of our new clients are interested in or need all five right away. They typically come in with only one or two initial concerns.

Then, when they have resolved those concerns, we can speak with them about the remaining elements of planning for their retirement. One meaning behind "Holistic" is that our clients have thought about — and we have written up for them— all five plans. All five are essential.

# Investment Customization

A few other unique attributes of our Strategic Diversification Services (SDS) are, as always, focused on customization for each client and the competitive performance of their investments.

The first customization is for our clients who want to focus investments in their areas of interest. Clients interested in areas such as biotech, information technology, health care, energy, or foreign stocks can bolster investments in those areas.

The second customization is tax-loss harvesting. This is for clients' non-retirement accounts. It is a way to extract losses when an asset class goes down without leaving the asset class.

By selling one instrument in that asset class and buying an identical one on the same day, clients do not lose the value but execute an on-the-books short-term or long-term capital loss. This is valuable in volatile times and for our tax-sensitive clients. In a word, it can help them *save* money at tax time. Most of our clients who have non-retirement assets tend to be tax sensitive. This process automatically executes tax loss harvesting on behalf of the client without any need for them to intervene.

# The McAdam "Spend, Protect, Grow" Model

As we have repeatedly demonstrated, if the age-old "4 Percent Rule" is no longer relevant, clients need a way to spend what they need and want in retirement while still having plenty of resources on the day they die.

We call this model "Spend, Protect, Grow" (SPG). It works by trifurcating client financial assets into three "buckets":

1. Spend: The amount they intend to spend (typically) over the next ten to twelve years
2. Protect: The amount they want to protect for as long as possible with no risk of loss due to market performance
3. Grow: The amount they hope to grow as much as possible to fight long-term inflation

## The Spend Bucket

First, we work with you to identify the amount of assets or spending you'll need for the next ten to twelve years based on the written retirement income plan from your fee-based financial planning.

Say we know your Spend amount will be $150,000 yearly after tax. The Spend Bucket cannot afford to incur any losses, so it is acceptable for the gains to be modest as long as they're consistent. The returns might be similar to a bank or financial institution's money market rates: around 3 to 5 percent, yet very stable.

At McAdam, we use a specific selection of financial instruments to fill this Spend Bucket to fund the first ten to twelve years of retirement. It is important to note that the Spend bucket is expected to be spent down until it is gone, which is a different paradigm and sometimes difficult for clients to accept at first. Once the Spend Bucket is set, we turn to the remaining two buckets.

## The Protect Bucket

The Protect Bucket is most easily defined as an agreed-upon amount of money you never want to lose. As such, it is best filled with what we call Safe Money Strategies (SMS). These investments are guaranteed not to lose money due to market performance while still providing the potential to grow.

It is a common misconception that Safe Money Strategies do not produce decent long-term returns — quite the contrary. Today, many approaches to SMS offer considerable upside while at the same time contractually guaranteeing no downside, regardless of underlying market performance. Any of our investors unfamiliar with this strategy always tend to be pleasantly surprised that SMS exist yet appropriately skeptical about how they could be possible.

Let's face it: For each client, the percentage that ought to be in the Protect Bucket may differ vastly from person to person, even those of a similar age and wealth demographic. This is primarily due to the variability in people's risk tolerance and life goals. For example, if a client knows their risk tolerance is seventy-thirty, this tells us that 70 percent of their invested assets beyond the Spend Bucket would be in the Grow Bucket while 30 percent would be in the Protect Bucket or SMS. We've even seen situations between spouses where one is seventy-thirty while the other is thirty-seventy. Rest assured; we take that into account.

Today, we use Safe Money Strategies where bonds were previously deployed. The conventional wisdom that bonds are a safe way to earn a reasonable rate of return has imploded. Our SMS are a safer way to earn similar (if not better) returns than typical bonds, bond funds, or bond exchange-traded funds (ETFs).

In summary, the Protect Bucket assets are Safe Money Strategies emanating from a client's comfortable risk tolerance. We discover and sometimes adjust this tolerance from the written retirement income plan. The amount in Protect versus Grow matches client goals and objectives with their resources to ensure they can achieve everything they want.

## The Grow Bucket

Last, we turn our attention to the remaining Grow Bucket. This is the "sexy" stuff, as they say.

This Bucket is filled with assets expected to go up significantly over the long run, even if they go down for periods of time. These are your high-flying stocks, mutual funds, ETFs, or other collections of equity-oriented assets that change in value daily.

Grow Bucket investments are meant to be held and evaluated over a long-term timeframe — say, ten years and beyond — and are expected to grow at the highest rate and fastest pace of the three buckets.

The beauty of designing a more aggressive Grow Bucket (to get higher long-term rates of return) is that patience is inherently built into the investment process. In retirement, clients can only have a Grow Bucket when they have solved the income issues for the more immediate timeframe with the Spend Bucket and when the Protect Bucket has some assets that simply should not lose value.

In other words, if you expect an asset class to increase over the long term but go through some difficult down periods along the way, you don't need to worry because you have the Spend and Protect assets set up. Having those allows the Grow Bucket to profit or experience a downturn over a long-term growth timeframe that most investors could not stomach along the way otherwise. It also distinctly avoids the need to withdraw assets from a pool that has gone down in value — a kiss of death in the quest to maintain enough assets for a lifetime and beyond.

Clients sometimes ask, "If the Spend Bucket is only for the next ten or so years, what happens when it ultimately runs out? We'll only be seventy-seven years old."

Here is the answer: Assets in the Protect and the Grow Buckets are redeployed into new SPG Buckets in another ten-to-twelve-year cycle.

This cyclical "rerun" is kicked off by reviewing and updating your entire written retirement income plan with up-to-date figures and life circumstances. Because it is data-driven, it is objective and, as with the original plan, considers your (perhaps updated) risk tolerance.

We advise clients to re-engineer their plans every ten to twelve years. This review process makes the McAdam SPG model a living, breathing financial security tool that, once executed, may still be adjusted along the way so that it serves you best.

# Tax Diversification and Asset Location

When our parents said, "Don't put all your eggs in one basket," they were essentially talking about *diversification*.

Tax diversification isn't about asset allocation (money in large-cap stocks or government bonds, which are asset *classes*). Instead — like that egg basket — tax diversification refers to asset *location* and *where* the money is saved or invested from a tax perspective.

When we save money, there are only three places (or locations) where we can put it from a tax standpoint. Each place is defined by how the money will be taxed *in the future* based on how it was or was not taxed *in the past*. Let me emphasize this: *please* consult your tax advisor regarding all matters of taxation. Our goal is to educate you so you know what to ask your tax advisor about.

## Understanding Tax Diversification

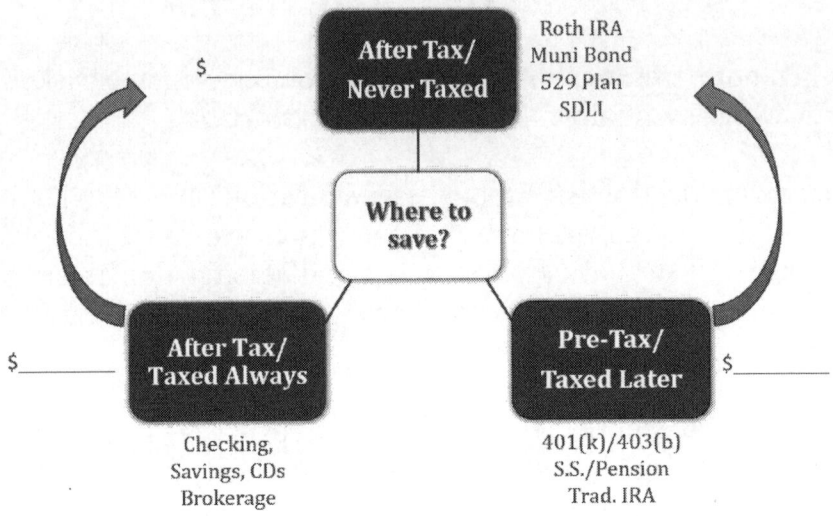

### *After Tax/Taxed Always (AT/TA)*

The first location investors put their money is in *"After Tax/Taxed Always."* These are dollars that go into accounts that can own most any financial instrument but are not considered "retirement accounts" (for example, bank or credit union checking accounts, savings accounts, money market accounts, CDs, or brokerage accounts). If those accounts earn some interest or dividends, we'll *always* pay the taxes on that earned money.

---

\* This is for conceptual and informational use only; this does not represent a recommendation to buy a specific product or investment. McAdam, LLC is not a tax advisory firm. Thus, this does not constitute tax advice. Any tax decisions should be made with your tax professionals. Proceeds from a life insurance policy are generally tax-free as per section 7702 of the US tax code. Past performance does not guarantee future results, and your results will vary.

The slight wrinkle here is whether those assets are capital-gain-oriented. That means you'll only pay taxes when you sell them, but you will *always* be taxed at the time of sale. For this reason, we call them After Tax/Taxed Always.

### *Pre-Tax/Taxed Later (PT/TL)*

The next location for assets is called *"Pre-Tax/Taxed Later."* These are the not-yet-taxed dollars in your 401(k), 403(b), or traditional IRA, as well as your Social Security benefits and most pensions — vehicles mostly considered "retirement accounts."

Americans are deeply obsessed with this asset location because they love the idea of lowering their taxes right *now* — the year they are in. That's what conventional wisdom has told them to do. Doing it this way means no taxes are paid on the money saved or invested during the year it was earned and put into the pre-tax account. The money grows without that growth being taxed for years and often decades. When is it all taxed? Only when it's withdrawn. However, every penny of that money is taxable as "ordinary income" when it gets withdrawn — no matter how many years later that might be. The potential impact of this is widely underestimated by the underinformed.

### *After Tax/Never Taxed (AT/NT)*

The third location is the *"After Tax/Never Taxed."* We should say "rarely taxed," but in practice, rarely is pretty close to never. After Tax/Never Taxed consists of locations that are always funded with after-tax dollars but grow tax-free, like a Roth IRA. Municipal bonds invested in federal or state entities that produce tax-free dividends (but not including the capital gains inside them) are After Tax/Never Taxed. Also, 529 plans (a way to save for children's and grandchildren's education) provide preferential tax treatment where the growth of the 529 will not be taxed.

### *Specially Designed Life Insurance (SDLI)*

Last but not least, there is a poorly understood and little-known concept in the After Tax/Never Taxed location we call *"Specially Designed Life Insurance."* When properly designed, it falls squarely into this After Tax/Never Taxed category.

SDLI is a form of life insurance where you deliberately purchase as little death benefit as possible (for cost-efficiency) and then slowly shift after-tax money into it over time to build up cash value. All that cash value grows tax-deferred until later, and then, instead of withdrawing the money, you can *borrow* it out.

When you can take a loan from your own money offered at a 0 percent net cost, you can use it tax-free throughout your lifetime. This practice is protected by Section 7702 of the Internal Revenue Code and has not changed in almost forty years! When you die, the loan is forgiven (tax-free), and any remaining death benefit in the policy will go to your beneficiaries. That's going to be income-tax-free, too.

Why do you need to talk to us and learn about SDLI and the other options in this After Tax/Never Taxed location?

1. Very few financial instruments have the same advantages as SDLI, which can include death benefits, access to funds, non-taxable income during one's lifetime, long-term care protection riders, and income-tax-free death benefits, all conveniently situated on a single life insurance chassis.
2. SDLI is one of the last bastions of tax efficiency for our clients who have built up some wealth.
3. SDLI should not be structured by a typical money manager or an average life insurance salesperson. Design from an experienced professional is imperative due to the specialized nature of tax laws within the life insurance domain.

Deciding *when* and *how* to subscribe to this strategy is material to long-term tax success because so many people retire with significant assets in AT/TA and PT/TL. However, many have next to nothing in AT/NT instruments. This opens them to future heavy taxation — most notably the devaluation of their assets with a stroke of a pen if tax laws should change, as they often do. None of us in the profession has a crystal ball to know if, when, and by how much the tax laws and brackets might change in the near and distant future. However, let's look back at the highest marginal income tax brackets from the past 110 years — 1914 to 2024. As I write this book in 2024, the highest federal marginal income tax bracket is 37 percent. The historical average over those 110 years is actually 57 percent.

## U.S. Historical Top Marginal Income Tax Rates

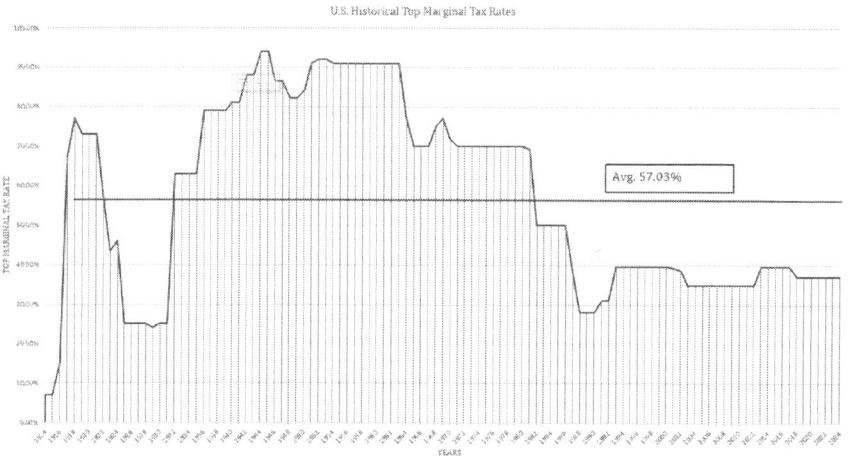

Average based on years 1914-2024.

\*

---

\* This is for conceptual and informational use only; this does not represent a recommendation to buy a specific product or investment. McAdam, LLC is not a tax advisory firm. Thus, this does not constitute tax advice. Any tax decisions should be made with your tax professionals.

That's a significant difference, and future changes in percentage can extensively diminish America's wealth in retirement.

# Potential Risks to Your Ideal Retirement

Ever feel like life gets in the way and prevents you from doing things you shouldn't ignore? I think if we're honest with ourselves, we've all put off obligations we know are important. Procrastination can be very costly. In your case, you may be reading this book because it's time to get serious about financial planning and, specifically, devising a way to ideally prepare for retirement. A retirement plan should be based on more components than just your investments or your finances. The preparation of that strategy begins with your desires, ambitions, and goals for this fulfilling season of life.

There's no such thing as a silly question — not when one of the most common questions we hear from folks regarding retirement is, "Am I going to be okay?" It often seems people are reluctant to meet with financial professionals because they worry they might sound uneducated. However, it's understandable for you to be a novice when it comes to financial issues and retirement concerns. You've been busy with your life and your career. Hopefully, time spent away from work has meant time spent being around those you love and engaging in the activities you enjoy. Retirement provides the opportunity to do even more of that while not fretting over work obligations.

Concerns people have about what they may encounter during retirement can be far-reaching and still perfectly legitimate. For a quick snapshot, I want to provide a brief sampling of wide-ranging issues that can come up during discussions about what to potentially brace for in retirement. This book will touch on many of these issues in further detail.

**Politics:** A presidential election often stirs emotions regarding potential effects on the economy. Investors grow anxious about how a new president can influence market returns. It's Congress, however, that establishes tax laws and passes spending bills. Yet the president can indirectly affect the economy and the stock market in various ways, such as the appointment of policymakers, development of international relations, and influential sway on new legislation.

**Taxes:** An example of a president's influence can be cited in signature legislation passed during Donald Trump's presidency, the Tax Cuts and Jobs Act of 2017. However, our tax system remains progressive, so the more you earn, the higher the tax rate within each tax bracket of subsequently higher income. A thorough understanding of tax regulations can be very beneficial. A financial professional can help identify potential tax planning issues a tax professional can help solve.

**Inflation:** General increases in the prices of goods and services, as measured by the consumer price index (CPI), often stem from fluctuations in real demand for goods and services. Inflation can discourage investment, which in turn can cause shortages in goods. A retiree's income can be impacted by the effect inflation can have on a fixed budget. The value of currency decreases because inflation erodes purchasing power.

**Cybersecurity:** Think you'll give up your smartphone in retirement? No way, right? It's here to stay, along with other intellectual gadgetry, including devices that have not been patented or invented yet. Retirees are becoming more tech-savvy, yet they can also be more trusting, which can be problematic when responding to potential scammers by phone, text, or email. Cybercrime often uses technology to target potential victims. Scammers, much like technology, figure to only grow more sophisticated over time.

# Risk and Its Effect on the Probability of Success

To adequately understand and minimize market risk, we build your plan using several kinds of tools.

The first is called a Monte Carlo simulation. It's designed to show clients how long their money might last depending on how they structure their finances, using prior data to simulate 1,000 possible outcomes.

We also use the Monte Carlo tool to simulate a bear market that might occur early in retirement right after completing our analysis.

Just as protecting against "sequence of returns" risk is vital, this is an essential part of the de-risking process. I will go into this a bit more in Chapter 11. The Bear Market Test takes the Monte Carlo simulations for your current and recommended plans and shows how a bear market would impact them.

The goal of this — and all our planning with you — is to show you the necessity of moving into a de-risked retirement portfolio that better protects your assets from risk and significant market volatility. Unless you stress test your current asset composition, you could fail to see how much risk you are exposed to in a bear market. For many of our clients, this is what their other advisors missed when only showing average rates of return. It may also be the only thing that could ruin an otherwise beautiful, long-term retirement if not addressed. *You cannot miss this step when de-risking your retirement portfolio.*

Knowledge about taxes, income, health care, investments, and leaving a legacy is key to writing up your retirement plan and helping you review it with your advisor over time. The following chapters present valuable information about the planning approach you'll need to consider before and during retirement.

I know some of this information can be overwhelming, so please check out the FAQ at the end of the book to help answer any remaining questions. You can also reach out to me directly at philsimonides@mcadamfa.com.

CHAPTER 1

# Longevity

You would think the prospect of the grave would loom more frightening as we age, yet many retirees say their number one concern is actually running out of money in their twilight years.[1] Unfortunately, this concern is justified because of one significant factor: We're living longer.

According to the Social Security Administration's 2011 Trustee Report, in 1950, the average life expectancy for a sixty-five-year-old man was seventy-eight, and the average for a sixty-five-year-old woman was eighty-one.[2] In the 2023 Trustees Report issued by the SSA, those averages were eighty-three and eighty-six, respectively.[3]

The bottom line of many retirees' budget woes comes down to this: They just didn't plan to live so long. Now, when we are younger and in our working years, that's not something we necessarily see as a bad thing; some people fantasize about living forever or, at least, reaching the ripe old age of 100!

---

[1] Brett Arends. MarketWatch. June 5, 2023. "Americans are 'more afraid of running out of money than death'" https://www.marketwatch.com/story/americans-are-more-afraid-of-running-out-money-than-death-ee5e22e9
[2] Social Security Administration. 2024. "Actuarial Publications: Cohort Life Expectancy" https://www.ssa.gov/oact/TR/2011/lr5a4.html
[3] Social Security Administration. 2023. "Period Life Expectancy — 2023 OASDI Trustees Report" https://www.ssa.gov/OACT/TR/2023/lr5a4.html

However, with a longer lifespan, we face a few snags as we retire. Our resources are finite — we only have so much money to provide income — but our lifespans can be unpredictably long, perhaps longer than our resources allow. Also, longer lives don't necessarily equate with healthier lives. The longer you live, the more money you will likely need to spend on health care, even if you don't include long-term care costs associated with nursing homes.

You will also run into inflation. If you don't plan to live another twenty-five years but end up doing so, inflation at an average of 3 percent will more than double the price of goods over that time period.

Because we don't necessarily get to have our cake and eat it, too, our collective increased longevity hasn't necessarily increased the healthy years of our lives. Typically, our life-extending care most widely applies to the time in our lives when we will need more care in general. Think of common situations like a pacemaker at eighty-five or cancer treatment at seventy-eight.

"Wow, Phil," I can hear you say. "Way to start with the good news first."

I know, I've painted a grim picture, but all I'm concerned about here is cost. It's hard to put a dollar sign on life, but that is essentially what we're talking about when discussing longevity and finances. Living longer isn't a bad thing; it just costs more, and one key to a sound retirement strategy is preparing for it in advance.

Here's a story of one woman that illustrates this picture perfectly. Her mother passed away in her late seventies after years of suffering from Alzheimer's disease. Her father died at eighty from cancer. With modern medicine and treatment, this woman survived two rounds of breast cancer, lived with diabetes, and relied on a pacemaker, extending her life to age eighty-eight — nearly a decade beyond what she anticipated. However, she and her husband had saved and planned for "just in case," trying to be prepared if they had to move, needed nursing home care, or needed to help children and grandchildren with their expenses.

One of their "just-in-case" scenarios was living much longer than they anticipated. The last six years of her life were fraught with medical expenses, but she was also blessed with knowing her five great-grandchildren and deepening relationships with her children and grandchildren. She was able to pay for her own medical care, including her final two years in a nursing home, and her twilight years were truly golden. From age eighty-five to eighty-eight, she was more socially active, with many visits from family and friends. She participated in more activities than she had in the seven years since her husband died. Her planning from decades earlier allowed her to pass on a legacy to her children when she passed away herself. The legacy she left behind can be measured both in dollar signs *and* in other intangible ways.[*]

Living longer may be more expensive, but it can be so meaningful when you plan for your "just-in-cases."

# Retiring Early

A key part of planning for retirement revolves around retirement income. After all, retirement is cutting the cord that tethers you to your employer — and your monthly check. However, that check often comes with many other benefits, particularly health care. Health care is often the thing that can unexpectedly put dreams for an early retirement on hold. Some employers offer health benefits to their retired workers, but

---

[*] This is a hypothetical example provided for illustrative purposes only; it does not represent a real-life scenario and should not be construed as advice designed to meet the particular needs of an individual's situation.

that number has declined drastically over the past several decades.

In 1988, among employers who offered health benefits to their workers, 66 percent offered health benefits to their retirees. That number has since dwindled to only 21 percent.[4] So, with employer-offered retirement health benefits on the wane, this has become a major point of concern for anyone who is looking to retire, particularly those who are looking to retire before age sixty-five, when they would become eligible for Medicare coverage.

Fidelity estimates that the average retired couple at age sixty-five will need approximately $315,000 for health care expenses in retirement, not including long-term care.[5] Do you think it's likely that cost will decrease?

Even if you are working until age sixty-five or have plans to cover your health expenses until that point, I often have clients who incorrectly assume Medicare is their golden ticket to cover all expenses. That is simply not the case. For example, Medicare only covers the first 100 days of "long-term care," after which people must rely on their assets or an LTC policy if they have one.

# Retiring Later

Planning for a long life in retirement partly depends on when you retire. While many people end up retiring earlier than they anticipated — due to injuries, layoffs, family crises, and other unforeseen circumstances — continuing to work past age sixty

4 Henry J. Kaiser Family Foundation. October 27, 2022. "2022 Employer Health Benefits Survey" https://www.kff.org/report-section/ehbs-2022-section-11-retiree-health-benefits/
5 Fidelity. June 21, 2023. "How to plan for rising health care costs" https://www.fidelity.com/viewpoints/personal-finance/plan-for-rising-health-care-costs

(and even sixty-five) is still a viable option for others and can be an excellent way to help establish financial confidence in retirement.

There are many reasons for this. For one, you obviously still earn a paycheck and the benefits accompanying it. Medical coverage and beefing up your retirement accounts with further savings can be significant by themselves, but continuing to generate income should also keep you from dipping into your retirement funds, further allowing them the opportunity to grow. When retirement accounts are at their peak, it's typical for people to underestimate the impact of the accounts' potential asset growth.

Additionally, for many workers, their nine-to-five job is more than just clocking in and out. Having a sense of purpose can keep us active physically, mentally, and socially. That kind of activity and level of engagement may also help stave off many of the health problems that plague retirees. Avoiding a sedentary life is one of the advantages of staying plugged into the workforce, if possible.

I recently ran into a friend named Joe at our golf club. I asked him whether he was finally retired now that he was in his late fifties, and we laughed about how he and his business partner Rob sold their company in their early forties for $41 million. They waited two years for a non-compete clause, and after buying enough cars and houses and navigating retirement life, they went back and opened a new company for twelve years — and then sold that one, too! They are now considering selling their third entity, but they always had plenty of money; they just saw what they were still capable of and wanted to do it!

I've also recently run into several people who seemed to have dialed back their work effort to a sustainable level, are being paid pretty well to do it, and find themselves not really hunkering to retire any time soon! I must admit that I feel more like this than I expected to myself as I turn sixty this year!

# CHAPTER 2

# Health Care

Take a second to reflect on your health care plan. Although working up to or even past age sixty-five could allow you to avoid a coverage gap between your working years and Medicare, that may not be an option for you. Even if it is, when you retire, you will need to make some decisions about what kind of insurance coverage you may need to supplement your Medicare. Are there any medical needs you have that may require coverage in addition to Medicare? Did your parents or grandparents have any inherited medical conditions you might consider using a special savings plan to cover?

These are all questions that are important to review with your financial professional so you can be sure you have enough money put aside for health care.

## Long-Term Care

Longevity means the need for long-term care is statistically more likely to happen. If you intend to pass on a legacy, planning for long-term care is paramount since most estimates project nearly 70 percent of Americans who reach age sixty-five will need some type of it.[6] However, this may be one of the biggest, most stressful pieces of longevity planning I encounter in my work. For one thing, who wants to talk about the point in their lives when they may feel the most limited? Who wants to dwell on what will happen if they can no longer toilet, bathe, dress, or feed themselves?

I get it; this is a less-than-fun part of planning. But a little bit of preparation now can go a long way!

When it comes to your longevity, just like with your goals, one of the important things to do is sit and dream. It may not be the fun, road-trip-to-the-Grand-Canyon kind of dreaming, but you can spend time envisioning how you want your twilight years to look.

For instance, if it is important for you to live in your home for as long as possible, who will provide for the day-to-day fixes and to-dos of housework if you become ill? Will you set aside money for a service, or do you have relatives or friends nearby you could comfortably allow to help you? Do you prefer in-home care over a nursing home or assisted living? Most people do. This could be a good time to discuss the possibility of moving into a retirement community versus staying where you are or whether it's worth moving to another state and leaving family, friends, and your entire social ecosystem behind.

These are all important factors to discuss with your spouse and children, as *now* is the right time to address questions and concerns. For instance, is aging in place more important to one spouse than the other? Are the friends or relatives who live nearby emotionally, physically, and financially capable of

---

[6] Claire Samuels. A Place for Mom. September 13, 2023. "Long-Term Care Statistics: A Portrait of Americans in Assisted Living, Nursing Homes, and Skilled Nursing Facilities" https://www.aplaceformom.com/senior-living-data/articles/long-term-care-statistics

helping you for a time if you face an illness? Do you want them to feel as though they would have to?

Many families I meet with find these conversations very uncomfortable, particularly when adult children discuss nursing home care with their parents. A knee-jerk reaction for many is to promise they will care for their aging parents. This is noble and well-intentioned, but there needs to be an element of realism here. Does "help" from an adult child mean they stop by and help you with laundry, cooking, home maintenance, and bills? Or does it mean they move you into their spare room when you have hip surgery? Are they prepared to help you use the restroom and bathe if that becomes difficult for you to do on your own?

I don't mean to discourage families from caring for their own; this can be a profoundly admirable relationship when it works out. However, I've seen families put off planning for late-in-life care based on a tenuous promise or assumption that the adult children would care for their parents, only to watch as the support system crumbles. Sometimes, this is because the assumed caregiver hasn't given serious thought to the preparation they would need, both in a formal sense and regarding their personal physical, emotional, and financial commitments. This is often also because we can't see the future: Alzheimer's disease, dementia, and other maladies of old age can exact a heavy toll. When a loved one reaches the point where they are at risk of wandering away or need help with two or more activities of daily living, it can be more than one person or a family can realistically handle.

If you know what you want, communicate with your family about both the best-case and worst-case scenarios. Then, hope for the best and plan for the worst.

## Realistic Cost of Care

Included in your planning should be a consideration for the cost of long-term care. The potential costs for such care and treatment can be underestimated, especially by those who have maintained robust health and find it difficult to envision future declines in their condition.

Another piece of planning for long-term care costs is anticipating inflation. It's common knowledge that prices have been and keep rising, which can lower your purchasing power on everything from food to medical care. Long-term care is a big piece of the inflation-disparity pie.

While local costs vary from state to state, the following table shows the national median for various forms of long-term care (plus projections that account for a 3 percent annual inflation, so you can see what I am referencing):[7]

---

[7] Nationwide. 2024. "Compare Long-term Care costs from state to state" https://nationwidefinancialltcmap.hvsfinancial.com/

| Long-Term Care Costs: Inflation | | | | |
|---|---|---|---|---|
| | Informal Care | Home Care | Assisted Living | Nursing Home (semi-private room) |
| Annual 2024 | $42,037 | $33,621 | $60,874 | $113,522 |
| Annual 2034 | $56,495 | $45,184 | $81,810 | $160,134 |
| Annual 2044 | $75,924 | $60,723 | $109,945 | $225,884 |
| Annual 2054 | $102,036 | $81,607 | $147,757 | $318,632 |

## Fund Your Long-Term Care

One common mistake I see occurs in those families who haven't planned for long-term care because they assume the government will provide everything. But that's a big misconception. The government has two health insurance programs: Medicare and Medicaid. These can greatly assist you in your health care *needs* in retirement but usually don't provide enough coverage to cover all your health care *costs* in retirement. My firm isn't a government outpost, so we don't get to make decisions regarding policy and specifics about either of these programs. I'm going to give an overview of both, but if you want to dive into the details of these programs, you can visit www.Medicare.gov and www.Medicaid.gov.

## Medicare

Medicare covers those aged sixty-five and older and those who are disabled. Medicare's coverage of any nursing-home-related health issues is limited. It might cover your nursing home stay if it is not a "custodial" stay and isn't long-term. For example, if you break a bone or suffer a stroke, stay in a nursing home for rehabilitative care, and then return home, Medicare may cover you. However, if you have developed dementia or are looking to move to a nursing facility because you can no longer bathe, dress, toilet, feed yourself, or take care of your hygiene, etc., then Medicare is not going to pay for your nursing home costs.[8]

You can enroll in Medicare anytime during the three months before and three months after your sixty-fifth birthday. Miss your enrollment deadline, and you could risk paying increased premiums for the rest of your life.[9] On top of prompt enrollment, there are a few other things to think about when it comes to Medicare, not least among them being the need to understand the different "parts," what they do, and what they don't cover.

### Part A

Medicare Part A is what you might think of as "classic" Medicare. Hospital care, some types of home health care, and major medical care fall under this. While most enrollees pay nothing for this service (as they likely paid into the system for at least ten years), you might have to, based on either work history or delayed signup. In 2024, the highest premium is $505 per month, and a hospital stay does have a deductible — $1,632.[10] Also, if you have a hospital stay that surpasses sixty days, you could be looking at additional costs; keep in mind, Medicare doesn't pay for long-term care and services.

---

[8] Medicare. 2024. "What Part A covers" https://www.medicare.gov/what-medicare-covers/what-part-a-covers
[9] Medicare. 2024. "When can I sign up for Medicare?" https://www.medicare.gov/basics/get-started-with-medicare/sign-up/when-can-i-sign-up-for-medicare
[10] Centers for Medicare & Medicaid Services. October 12, 2023. "2024 Medicare Parts A & B Premiums and Deductibles" https://www.cms.gov/newsroom/fact-sheets/2024-medicare-parts-b-premiums-and-deductibles?ref=biztoc.com

## Part B

Medicare Part B is an essential piece of wrap-around coverage for Medicare Part A. It helps pay for doctor visits and outpatient services. This also comes with a price tag: Although the Part B annual deductible is only $240 in 2024, you will still pay 20 percent of all costs after that, with no limit on out-of-pocket expenses. The Part B monthly premium for 2024 ranges from the standard amount of $174.70 to $594.[11]

## Part C

Medicare Part C (more commonly known as a Medicare Advantage plan) is an alternative to a combination of Parts A, B, and sometimes D. Administered through private insurance companies, these have a variety of costs and restrictions, and they are subject to the specific policies and rules of the issuing carrier.

## Part D

Medicare Part D is also offered through a private insurer and is supplemental to Parts A and B, as its primary purpose is to cover prescription drugs. Like any private insurance plan, Part D has its quirks and rules that vary from insurer to insurer.

## The Donut Hole

Even with a "Part D" in place, you may still have a coverage gap between what your Part D private drug insurance pays for your prescription and what basic Medicare pays. In 2024, the coverage gap is $5,030, meaning that after you meet your private prescription insurance limit, you will spend no more than 25 percent of your drug costs out-of-pocket before Medicare kicks in to pay for more prescription drugs.[12]

---

[11] Ibid.
[12] Medicare. 2024. "Costs in the coverage gap"
https://www.medicare.gov/drug-coverage-part-d/costs-for-medicare-drug-coverage/costs-in-the-coverage-gap

Note: In the donut hole, you pay up to 25 percent out of pocket for all covered medications. You leave the donut hole once you've spent $8,000 out of pocket for covered drugs in 2024. 2024 is the last year for the donut hole. A $2,000 out-of-pocket cap takes effect for Medicare Part D in 2025.

### *Medicare Supplements*

Medicare Supplement Insurance, MedSupp, Medigap, or plans labeled Medicare Part F, G, H, I, J ... Known by a variety of monikers, this is just a fancy way of saying "medical coverage for those over sixty-five that picks up the tab for whatever the federal Medicare program(s) doesn't." Again, costs, limitations, etc., vary by carrier.

Does that sound like a bunch of government alphabet soup to you? It certainly does to me. And did you read the fine print? Unpredictable costs, varied restrictions, difficult-to-compare benefits, donut holes, and coverage gaps. That's par for the course with health care plans throughout our adult lives. What gives? I thought Medicare was supposed to be easier, comprehensive, and at no cost!

The truth is there is probably no stage of life when health care is easy to understand.

One of the best things you can do for yourself is to scope out the health care field early, compare costs often, and prepare for out-of-pocket costs well in advance — decades, if possible.

## Medicaid

Medicaid is a program the states administer, so funding, protocol, and limitations vary. Compared to Medicare, Medicaid more widely covers nursing home care, but it targets a different demographic: those with low incomes.

If you have more assets than the Medicaid limit in your state and need nursing home care, you will need to use those assets to pay for your care. Fortunately, you will find a list of additional state-approved ways to use or spend some of these assets over the Medicaid limit, such as pre-purchasing burial plots and funeral expenses or paying off debts. After that, your remaining assets fund your nursing home stay until they are gone, at which point Medicaid will jump in.

Some people aren't stymied by this, thinking they will just pass on their financial assets early by gifting them to relatives, friends, and causes so they can qualify for Medicaid when they need it. However, to prevent this exact scenario, Uncle Sam has implemented what's called the "look-back period." Currently, if you enroll in Medicaid, you are subject to having the government scrutinize the last five years of your finances for large gifts or expenses that may subject you to penalties, temporarily making you ineligible for Medicaid coverage.

So, if you're planning to preserve your money for future generations and retain control of your financial resources during your lifetime, you'll probably want to prepare for the costs of longevity beyond a "government plan."

### *Self-Funding*
One way to fund a longer life is the old-fashioned way, through self-funding. There are a variety of financial tools you can use, and they all have their pros and cons. If your assets are in low-interest financial vehicles (savings, bonds, CDs), you risk letting inflation erode the value of your dollar. If you are relying on the stock market, you have more growth potential, but you'll also want to consider the possible implications of market volatility. What if your assets take a hit? If you suffer a loss in your retirement portfolio in early or mid-retirement, you might have the option to "tighten your belt," so to speak, and cut back on discretionary spending to allow your portfolio the room to bounce back. But if you are retired and depend on income from

a stock account that just hit a downward stride, what are you going to do? There is a better way! It's the Spend, Protect, Grow Model described in the opening chapter, The Importance of Planning.

### Health Savings Accounts (HSAs)

These days, you might also be able to self-fund through a health savings account if you have access to one through a high-deductible health plan (you will not qualify to save in an HSA after enrolling in Medicare). In an HSA, any growth of your tax-deductible contributions will be tax-free, and any distributions paid out for qualified health costs are also tax-free. Long-term care expenses count as health costs, so if this is an option available to you, it is one way to use the tax advantages to self-fund your longevity. Bear in mind if you are younger than sixty-five, any money you use for non-qualified expenses will be subject to taxes and penalties, and if you are older than sixty-five, any HSA money you use for non-medical expenses is subject to income tax.

### Long-Term Care Insurance (LTCI)

One slightly more nuanced way to pay for longevity — specifically for long-term care — is long-term care insurance. As car insurance protects your assets in case of a car accident and home insurance protects your assets in case something happens to your house, long-term care insurance aims to protect *all* of your assets in case you need long-term care in an at-home or nursing home scenario.

As with other types of insurance, you will pay a monthly or annual premium in exchange for an insurance company paying for long-term care down the road. Typically, policies cover three to four years of care, which is adequate for an "average" situation: it's estimated that 70 percent of Americans aged sixty-five and older will need long-term care of some kind.[13]

Now, there are a few oft-cited components of LTCI that make it unattractive for some:

- Expense — LTCI can be expensive. It is generally less expensive the younger you are, but a sixty-five-year-old couple who purchased LTCI in 2023 could expect to pay a combined annual amount of $3,750 for a modest policy. And the annual cost only increases from there the older you are.[14] (It is important to note that this example may be on the low end for where you live. Most couples want to seek care close to home for all the reasons you can imagine. Get to know the costs in your area.)
- Limited options — LTCI may be expensive for consumers, but it can also be expensive for companies that offer it. With fewer companies willing to take on that expense, the market has narrowed, meaning opportunities to price shop for policies with different options or custom benefits are limited.
- If you know you need it, you might not be able to get it — Insurance companies offering LTCI are taking on a risk that you may need LTCI. That risk is the foundation of the product — you may or may not need it. If you know you will need it because you have a dementia diagnosis or another illness for which you will need long-term care, you will likely not qualify for LTCI coverage.

---

[13] Claire Samuels. A Place for Mom. September 13, 2023. "Long-Term Care Statistics: A Portrait of Americans in Assisted Living, Nursing Homes, and Skilled Nursing Facilities" https://www.aplaceformom.com/senior-living-data/articles/long-term-care-statistics

[14] American Association for Long-Term Care Insurance. 2023. "Long-Term Care Insurance Facts – Data – Statistics – 2023 Reports" https://www.aaltci.org/long-term-care-insurance/learning-center/ltcfacts-2023.php

- Use it or lose it — If you have LTCI and are in the minority of Americans who die having never needed long-term care, all the money you paid into your LTCI policy is gone.
- Possibly fluctuating rates — Your premium rate is not locked in on many LTCI policies. Companies maintain the ability to raise or lower your premium amounts. This means some seniors face an ultimatum: Keep funding a policy at what might be a less affordable rate *or* lose coverage and let go of all the money they have paid so far.

After that, you might be thinking, "How can people possibly be interested in LTCI?" But let me repeat myself — it's anticipated that as many as 70 percent of Americans will need long-term care. And although only one in ten Americans aged fifty-five-plus has purchased LTCI, keep in mind the high cost of nursing home care. Can you afford over $9,000 a month to put into nursing home care and still have enough left over to help protect your legacy? This is a genuine concern, not only because of the aforementioned statistic about long-term care needs but also because nearly a third of American seniors have some level of cognitive impairment — including 10 percent who have dementia.[15] So, not to sound like a broken record, but it is vitally important to have a plan in place to deal with longevity and long-term care, especially if you intend to leave a financial legacy.

On a positive note, a more modern style of LTCI has captured the interest of those concerned about some of the unattractive components I just listed. A few terrific programs address three main issues:

---

[15] Peter Urban. AARP. November 1, 2022. "1 in 10 Older Americans Have Dementia" https://www.aarp.org/health/brain-health/info-2022/cognitive-impairment-trends-in-older-americans.html

1. "What if I never need it?"
2. "What if I want to cancel it?"
3. "What if the cost changes too much as I get older?"

There is now a way to purchase LTCI inside a universal life insurance wrapper, which can guarantee coverage and pay an agreed-upon specified amount (death benefit) should you die without using it for LTC costs. Many of these newer hybrid products even allow you to cancel them and receive 70 percent of your premiums back at any time. Name one style of insurance you are familiar with that does those things! For the insurance company to keep these promises, you either pay them in one lump sum or evenly over ten years. This way, nothing is left to chance. This method has become quite popular for our clients, particularly those with financial assets they can liquidate to pay the premium and remove the risk for life!

We owe it to our clients to show the risks of LTC costs in their financial modeling for retirement, as well as this more modern LTCI solution, which addresses all of the traditional complaints people have about these care programs. The way our clients see it is that they can use a small amount of money to protect a much larger amount later!

A few relevant statistics to keep in mind:

- The longer you live, the more health care you will likely need to pay for.
- The median cost of a private nursing home room in the United States between 2022 and 2023 was $9,034 a month.[16] But keep in mind that is just the nursing home

---

[16] Merritt Whitley. A Place for Mom. May 19, 2023. "How Much Do Nursing Homes Cost? A State-By-State Guide" https://www.aplaceformom.com/caregiver-resources/articles/nursing-homes-cost

— it doesn't include other medical costs, let alone pleasantries like entertainment or hobby spending.
- As referenced earlier, Fidelity calculated in a 2022 study that a healthy couple retiring at age sixty-five could expect to pay around $315,000 over the course of retirement to cover health and medical expenses.

I know. "Whoa, there, Phil, I was hoping to have a realistic idea of health costs, not be driven over by a cement mixer!"

The good news is, while we don't know these exact costs in advance, we know there *will* be costs. And you won't have to pay your total Medicare lifetime premiums in one day as a lump sum. Now that you have a good idea of health care costs in retirement, you can *plan* for them! That's the real point here: Planning in advance can keep you from feeling nickel-and-dimed to your wits' end. Instead, having a sizeable portion of your assets earmarked for health care can allow you the freedom to choose health care networks, coverage options, and long-term care possibilities that you like.

### Product Riders

LTCI and self-funding are not the only ways to plan for the expenses of longevity. Some companies are getting creative with their products, particularly insurance companies. One way they are retooling to meet people's needs is through optional product riders on annuities and life insurance. Elsewhere in this book, I talk about annuity basics, but here's a brief overview: Annuities are issued by insurance companies. You pay the insurance company a premium — either as a lump sum or as a series of payments over a set amount of time — in exchange for certain investment qualities and perhaps guaranteed income payments, should you desire them.

One of the advantages of some annuities is that they may have access to riders, which allow you to tweak your contract for a fee — usually about 0.1 percent to 1 percent of the contract value per year.[17] One annuity rider some companies offer is a long-term care rider. If you have an annuity with a long-term care rider and are not in need of long-term care over the time you have it, your contract behaves as any annuity contract would — nothing changes. Suppose you reach a point when you can't perform multiple functions of daily life on your own (generally, this threshold is recognized as being unable to perform two of the six activities of daily living, or ADLs). In that case, you would notify the insurance company, and if you meet the long-term care rider requirements, your additional rider benefits can be activated to help you pay for your long-term care needs. An insurance company representative (or perhaps your advisor) will turn on those provisions of your contract. Activating LTC rider benefits is more involved than simply calling your insurance carrier. A physician has to confirm that you cannot perform the required amount of activities of daily living (ADLs).

Like LTCI, different companies and products offer different options. Some annuity long-term care riders offer coverage of two years in a nursing home situation. Others cap expenses at two times the original annuity's value. It greatly depends. Some people prefer this option because there isn't a "use-it-or-lose-it" piece; if you die without ever having needed long-term care, you still will have had both the investment and potentially the income benefit from the base contract.

Still, as with any annuities or insurance contracts, there are the usual restrictions and limitations. Withdrawing money from the contract will affect future income payments, early distributions can result in a penalty, income taxes may apply, and because the insurance company's solvency is what guarantees your payments, it's important to do your research

---

[17] Shawn Plummer. The Annuity Expert. 2024. "Annuity Fees: What You Need To Know" https://www.annuityexpertadvice.com/types-of-annuities/annuity-fees/

about the insurance company you are considering purchasing a contract from or hire a financial professional to do it for you. It's also important to note that some of today's life insurance products offer LTC riders at no additional cost — this is one way some insurers can increase their competitive advantage in a demanding marketplace.

Understandably, a discussion on long-term care is bound to feel at least a little tedious. Yet, this is an important piece of planning for income in retirement, particularly if you want to leave a legacy.

# Spousal Planning

Here's one thing to keep in mind no matter how you plan to save: Many of us will be planning for more than ourselves. Look back at all the stats on health events and the likelihood of long life and long-term care. If they hold true for a single individual, then the likelihood of having a costly health or long-term care event is even higher for a married couple. You'll be planning for not just one life but two. If one spouse stays at home while the other must go to an LTC facility, they should consider the new costs in addition to those of maintaining a home. So, when it comes to long-term care insurance, annuities, self-funding, or whatever strategy you are looking at using, be sure you are funding longevity for the both of you.

CHAPTER 3

# Taxes

When it comes to taxes, there are a few things most people agree on. One is that we all bear some responsibility, as Americans, to pay some share of federal income taxes needed to run the country and provide resources and services for our citizens. I often hear people say they are okay with paying their fair share of taxes. The issue arises when people unwittingly pay more than their fair share without realizing it. Even if they do, they are unsure what to do about it.

For most people, April conjures up images of the laborious process of getting documents together to send to their accountants or taking a weekend to do them on their own. The typical relationship between client and accountant is purely transactional and, as such, is inherently reactive. You send them all your stuff, and they tell you what you owe or what your refund is. There is only so much your accountant can do once the year has closed, yet this pattern has remained unchanged for decades. What most people would want (if they knew they could get it) is a process to help them proactively keep more of what they make each and every year. Therein lies the difference between accountants and financial advisors. An accountant is a tax *preparer*, and we are tax *planners*. What people really need is both — they just don't know it.

What I mean is tax planning extends beyond filing taxes. In April, we are required to settle our accounts with the IRS to make sure we have paid up on our bill or even the score if we have overpaid. But real tax planning is about making each financial move in a way that allows you to keep the most money in your pocket and out of Uncle Sam's. I always tell my clients, "Stop worrying about what you might pay in taxes this year and play the long game. Done correctly, you can pay way less in taxes in the long run – that should be your focus, especially throughout retirement."

Now, as a caveat, I want to emphasize I am neither a CPA nor a tax advisor, but I see the way taxes affect my clients, and I have plenty of experience helping clients implement tax-efficient strategies in their retirement plans in conjunction with their tax professionals.

# The Fed

Now, in the United States, taxes can be a rather uncertain proposition. Depending on who is in the White House and which party controls Congress, we might be tempted to assume tax rates could either decline or increase in the next four to eight years accordingly. However, there is one (large!) factor we, as a nation, must confront: the national debt.

Currently, according to USDebtClock.org, we are over $35,000,000,000,000 in debt and climbing. That's $35 *trillion* with a "T." With just $1 trillion parked in a bank at a zero percent interest rate, you could spend more than $54 million every day for fifty years without hitting a zero balance! That's hard to fathom.

Even if Congress got a handle on that debt and stopped its daily compound, divided by each taxpayer, we would each owe about $272,000. So, will that be check, cash, or Venmo?[18]

My point here isn't to give you anxiety. I'm just cautioning you that even with the rosiest of outlooks on our personal income tax rates, none of us should count on low tax rates for the long term. Instead, you and your network of professionals (tax, legal, and financial) should constantly be looking for ways to take advantage of tax-saving opportunities as they come.

So, how can we get started?

# Know Your Limits

One of the foundational pieces of tax planning is knowing and understanding your marginal tax rate. Marginal tax rate is the tax rate you pay on your highest dollar of income. In the United States, we use a progressive tax system, meaning your marginal tax rate increases as your taxable income increases. However, to be clear, not all of your income is taxed at that highest rate — only the upper portion.

A taxpayer's income is divided into tax brackets, and the brackets determine the rate applied to increments of the filer's taxable income.

For example, assume your married friends, Mike and Cindy, tell you their annual taxable income is $250,000. For married filing joint taxpayers, that income puts them in the 24 percent tax bracket, meaning the highest portion of their income is taxed at 24 percent, but other chunks of their income are taxed at lower rates. Using the 2024 tax bracket below, we can see their first $23,200 of income will be taxed at 10 percent, but

---

[18] https://www.usdebtclock.org. Accessed on November 13, 2024.

their next tranche of income ($23,201 to $94,300) will be taxed at 12 percent, and the next tranche ($94,301 to $201,050) at 22 percent. Finally, above $201,051, the remainder of their income will be taxed at 24 percent. Their tax owed for the year — before any additional taxes or credits — is the accumulation of those four amounts. In short, their income falls between $201,051 and $383,900 in the chart, so their tax is $34,337 plus 24 percent of the amount over $201,050.

| 2024 Tax Brackets: Married Filing Joint Filers | | |
|---|---|---|
| **Tax Rate** | **Taxable Income Bracket** | **Tax Owed** |
| 10% | $0 to $23,200 | 10% of taxable income. |
| 12% | $23,201 to $94,300 | $2,320 plus 12% of the amount over $23,200 |
| 22% | $94,301 to $201,050 | $10,852 plus 22% of the amount over $94,300 |
| 24% | $201,051 to $383,900 | $34,337 plus 24% of the amount over $201,050 |
| 32% | $383,901 to $487,450 | $78,221 plus 32% of the amount over $383,900 |
| 35% | $487,451 to $731,200 | $111,357 plus 35% of the amount over $487,450 |
| 37% | $731,201 or more | $196,669.50 plus 37% of the amount over $731,200 |

The 2024 bracket for single filers is presented below for comparison. Note that there are also unique brackets for married filing separately and head of household filers.

| 2024 Tax Brackets: Single Filers | | |
|---|---|---|
| **Tax Rate** | **Taxable Income Bracket** | **Tax Owed** |
| 10% | $0 to $11,600 | 10% of taxable income. |
| 12% | $11,601 to $47,150 | $1,160 plus 12% of the amount over $11,600 |
| 22% | $47,151 to $100,525 | $5,426 plus 22% of the amount over $47,150 |
| 24% | $100,526 to $191,950 | $17,168.50 plus 24% of the amount over $100,525 |
| 32% | $191,951 to $243,725 | $39,110.50 plus 32% of the amount over $191,950 |
| 35% | $243,726 to $609,350 | $55,678.50 plus 35% of the amount over $243,725 |
| 37% | $609,351 or more | $183,647.25 plus 37% of the amount over $609,350 |

[19]

It's important to note the difference between marginal and effective tax rates. The effective tax rate represents the percentage of taxable income an individual pays in taxes. To calculate the effective rate, take the total dollar amount you pay

---

[19] Sabrina Parys and Tina Orem. NerdWallet. April 15, 2024. "2023 and 2024 Tax Brackets and Federal Income Tax Rates" https://www.nerdwallet.com/article/taxes/federal-income-tax-brackets

in income tax and divide it by your total taxable income. Thus, it is the *average* tax rate and will always be a lower percentage than the marginal tax rate for anyone above the lowest bracket.

Why are marginal and effective rates important in retirement planning? Federal income tax is one of the biggest expenses individuals pay in their lives. In many cases, the lifetime amount can exceed a lifetime of mortgage payments. Although there are federal tax breaks for Americans over the age of sixty-five, many former high-income earners continue to pay substantial income taxes. Awareness of your marginal tax rate is one of the considerations in determining when to begin Social Security and an important factor in assessing potential Roth IRA conversion pacing. Also, a thorough analysis of current and future marginal tax rates is important in the strategic planning for required minimum distributions (RMDs) on pre-tax, deferred retirement accounts. We commonly refer to this process as *strategic distribution planning* (SDP), which aims to discover the most efficient use and distribution of resources, net of taxes over one's lifetime. Most of my clients didn't know what this was, but once articulated, they knew they wanted it!

## Assuming a Lower Tax Rate

Retirement has always been imagined as a time when you stop working and no longer earn wages or self-employment income. In the past, Social Security benefits were not subject to taxation. Even though pensions were usually taxable, their income stream didn't fully replace a recipient's previous salary. If they needed to pull from after-tax investment funds during retirement, that principal had already been taxed. In general, prior to the 1970s, income during retirement — cash inflow – was usually taxed at a lower rate than when people were working because they had less income, and certain portions of it were not taxable.

In 1978, lawmakers created Section 401 of the Internal Revenue Code to prevent companies from using tax-advantaged profit-sharing plans to primarily benefit executives. However, businessman Ted Benna reimagined this code as the foundation of the modern 401(k). This innovation ultimately led to the decline of traditional company pension plans while shifting both control and risk to employees. The most significant change was the shift of taxation from when employees were paid and when investment income was earned to taxation at the time of withdrawal. This tax advantage encouraged individuals to save more money in pre-tax, tax-deferred plans than they would have in regular savings accounts, up to the allowed limits.

In addition, in 1983, Social Security introduced new tax brackets to address the problem of decreasing reserves. This resulted in both the potential for Social Security to become taxable and a significant shift in retirement planning strategy. Within a five-year period, the retirement planning landscape changed for decades going forward, possibly forever.

A big selling point for qualified retirement accounts (401(k)s, 403(b)s, IRAs, etc.) has been the theory that people will pay less in taxes during their retirement years than during their working years when they're putting that money away. The idea is that you're allowed to "defer" paying the tax on that income until your marginal tax rate drops in retirement. Hence, you would pay less in tax on that income.

But what if it doesn't pan out that way? Some retirees' marginal tax rates will stay the same in retirement or even increase. If you have a healthy balance in your qualified retirement account, combining its RMDs or even a Roth conversion with Social Security can result in what is called the "tax torpedo." This tax increase occurs when a larger percentage of your Social Security becomes taxable, and that same income increase consequently bumps a taxpayer up to a higher marginal rate.

# 401(k)s/IRAs/Roth IRAs

One sometimes-unexpected piece of tax planning in retirement concerns the 401(k) or IRA. Most of us have one of these accounts or an equivalent. We pay in throughout our working lives, dutifully socking away a portion of our earnings in these tax-deferred accounts. There's the rub: tax-*deferred*, not tax-*free*. Very rarely is anything free of taxation when you get down to it. Using 401(k)s and IRAs to provide income in retirement is no different. The taxes the government deferred when you were in your working years are due when you withdraw the funds, and you will pay taxes on that income at whatever your current tax rate is.

Just to ensure Uncle Sam gets his due, the government also has a required minimum distributions (RMD) rule. Beginning at age seventy-three (or seventy-five if you were born in 1960 or after), you are required to withdraw a certain minimum amount every year from your 401(k) or IRA, or else you will face a tax penalty on any RMD monies you should have withdrawn but didn't — and that's on top of the requisite income tax owed. The SECURE Act 2.0 reduced the penalty to 25 percent (from 50 percent). Timely corrections also can further reduce the penalty to 10 percent.[20]

Of course, there is also the Roth IRA account. You can think of the difference between a Roth and a traditional retirement account as the difference between taxing the seed and taxing the harvest. Because Roths are funded with after-tax dollars, there aren't tax penalties for early withdrawals of the principal, nor are there taxes on the growth after you reach age fifty-nine-and-one-half. Perhaps best of all, there are no RMDs. Of course,

---

[20] Jim Probasco. Investopedia. October 20, 2023. "SECURE 2.0 Act of 2022: Overview, Rules, Limits" https://www.investopedia.com/secure-2-0-definition-5225115

you must own a Roth account for a minimum of five years before you are able to take advantage of all its features.

This is one more area where it pays to be aware of your marginal income tax rate. Some people may opt to put any excess RMDs from their traditional retirement accounts into stocks or insurance. Others may find it advantageous to "convert" their traditional retirement account funds to Roth account funds in a year during which they are in a lower tax bracket.

# Roth IRA Conversions

A Roth conversion simply means converting (or withdrawing) monies from your traditional, tax-deferred retirement accounts and moving them to a Roth account. Once inside the Roth, any growth on these funds will accumulate completely tax-free, and tax will not be owed when the Roth funds are withdrawn, assuming the conditions noted above. This is an exciting opportunity for accumulation! However, a thoughtful strategy is beneficial in the conversion process. Since dollars were placed into the traditional account pre-tax and the growth is taxable in these accounts, income tax is owed on *all* the money converted to the Roth. Converting an employer plan account to a Roth IRA is also a taxable event. Increased taxable income from the Roth IRA conversion may have several consequences, including (but not limited to) a need for additional tax withholding or estimated tax payments, the loss of certain tax deductions and credits, higher taxes on Social Security benefits, and higher Medicare premiums.

Points to consider regarding a conversion:

**How are you going to pay the tax?** Again, any time you withdraw funds from a 401(k) or traditional IRA, tax is owed on 100 percent of that money, whether the distribution was a basic withdrawal, an RMD, or a Roth conversion. In addition to the income tax, if the account owner is younger than fifty-nine-and-one-half, it is most likely a 10 percent tax penalty will be assessed. So, if you're under fifty-nine-and-one-half and have a year when your income is lower – reducing your marginal tax rate – you need to weigh the amount of the tax penalty against the decrease in ordinary income tax.

As a tricky sidenote, if you are under fifty-nine-and-one-half and you have tax withheld from your conversion and sent directly to the government, you will not escape the 10 percent penalty.

**Did you compare your current tax rate to your estimated future rate?** As mentioned above, a good time to consider a Roth is in a year when your taxable income — and thus your marginal tax rate — is lower than normal or lower than expected in the future. A popular conversion strategy is to transfer funds during a period referred to as "the trough years." That is the period after you've retired but before you begin receiving Social Security or are required to begin RMDs. It is easier to manage the tax on the conversion during these years as you have more control over the sources and the amounts of your income.

**What is your Roth withdrawal strategy?** There are four considerations here.

- Can you leave converted money in the Roth for at least five years? You must leave your converted money in the Roth for at least five years for the withdrawals to be tax-free. That five-year countdown begins on January 1 of the year you made the conversion, even if your conversion date was December 31. This five-year countdown applies in each year you make a conversion.

- Even if you hold the Roth funds for five years, you will still face penalties for withdrawals if you're under fifty-nine-and-one-half.[21]
- Once the account has been established for five years, new conversion amounts (for which conversion taxes are paid) are not subject to further tax right away, yet their earnings still need to age five years to be fully tax-free.
- The longer you leave funds inside the Roth after the conversion, the more time it can grow and potentially offset the tax levied on your traditional account's withdrawals. Remember, this money is now growing tax-free. A long growth period may be able to outweigh a loss in your balance due to income taxes owed at conversion time. Also, an error in overestimating future tax rates (i.e., your future rates turned out to be less than the conversion year) can be made up by holding funds in your Roth for many years.[22]
- Planning to use your Roth as a legacy planning tool? There are various rules and options depending on the type of heir, but in most cases, the Roth is given additional time to grow tax-free.

Does that make your head spin? Understandable. That's why it's so important to work with a financial professional and tax planner who can help you execute these sorts of tax-efficient strategies and help you understand what you are doing and why. The way we see it, anything you don't pay in taxes becomes

---

[21] Kailey Hagen. The Motley Fool. November 16, 2022. "4 Things to Know If You're Considering a Roth IRA Conversion This Year"
https://www.fool.com/retirement/2022/11/16/4-things-to-know-if-youre-considering-a-roth-ira-c/
[22] Tim Steffen. Baird Private Wealth Management. October 16, 2023. "The Three Tests Before a Roth Conversion"
https://www.bairdwealth.com/insights/wealth-management-perspectives/2023/09/the-three-tests-before-a-roth-conversion/

part of the lifetime resources you can use toward your specific goals. As always, I conclude by asking you to please consult your tax advisor.

# CHAPTER 4

# Market Volatility

U p and down. Roller coaster. Merry-go-round. Bulls and bears. Peak-to-trough.

Sound familiar? This is the language we use to talk about the stock market. With volatility and spikes, even our language is jarring, bracing, and vivid.

Still, many financial strategies tend to revolve around market-based products, and for good reasons. For one thing, there is no other financial class that packs the same potential for growth, pound for pound, as stock-based products. Because of growth potential, inflation challenges, and new opportunities, it may be disadvantageous to avoid the market entirely.

However, along with the potential for growth is the potential for loss. At the time this book was written, many of the people I've met with came in feeling uneasy because of the economic fallout of the COVID-19 outbreak of 2020, followed by the economic downturn and the inflation spike that happened in 2022. Despite 2023 being a comeback year in equities and 2024 bringing more all-time highs in the market, people still fear what may come next.

So, how do we balance these factors? How do we try to satisfy both the need for protection and the need for growth?

For one thing, it is important to recognize the value of diversification. Now, I'm not just talking about the diversifying of assets among different kinds of stocks, or even different kinds of stocks and bonds. That's only one kind of diversification. Stocks and bonds, though different, are both still important market-based products. Even within a diversified portfolio, most market-based products tend to rise or fall as a whole, just like an incoming tide. Therefore, a portfolio invested in only market-sourced products won't automatically preserve your assets during times when the market declines.

In addition to the sort of "horizontal diversification" you have by purchasing a variety of stocks and bonds from different companies, I also suggest you think about "vertical diversification," or layering diversification among asset classes. This means having different product types, including securities products, bank products, and insurance products — with varying levels of growth potential, liquidity, and protection — all in accordance with your unique situation, goals, and needs. The preponderance of safe money strategies available today can be critical in successfully balancing a portfolio for retirement.

One of my favorite stories about risk tolerance and volatility involves meeting with Greg and Sandy after one of my seminars. They were high school sweethearts now in their early sixties, and they wanted to discuss risk. I was talking to Greg about it and asked if he could estimate how much he would be willing to lose in one year in the market. He thought about it for a moment and then said, "I think about 10 percent," at which point Sandy burst out laughing and asked, "Did he say 10 percent, Phil!? Well, he meant to say ten *bucks*! This guy doesn't want to lose anything. I'm pretty sure he has money buried in a coffee can in the yard."

When she was asked the same question, Sandy said 20 percent. So, I asked them if they knew what their one-year potential risk of loss percentage currently was. Blank stares — and they already had an advisor! I asked if they would like me to do a risk analysis for them. Wouldn't you know it? Their number was more like a 40 percent one-year risk. To make a long story short, we immediately made changes to bring their investments more in line with their risk tolerance. And not a moment too soon — that was in 2021, and the stock and bond markets both went down quite a bit the following year. However, Greg and Sandy were way more protected than they had been as a direct result of our discussion and the work we did.

# The Color of Money

When you're looking at the overall diversification of your portfolio, part of the equation is knowing which products fit in what category: what has liquidity, what has asset protection, and what has growth potential.

Before we dive in, keep in mind these aren't absolutes. You might think of liquidity, growth, and asset protection as colors. While some products will look pretty much yellow, green, or blue, others will have a mix of characteristics, making them more orange, teal, or purple.

## Growth

I like to think of the growth category as green. It's powerful, it's somewhat volatile, and it's also the category where we have the greatest opportunities for growth and loss. Often, products in the growth category will have a good deal of liquidity but very little protection. These are our market-based products and strategies, and we think of them mostly in shades of green to designate their growth and liquidity. This is usually a good place to be when you're young — think fast cars and flashy clothing — but its allure often wanes as you move closer to retirement. Examples of "green" products include:

- Stocks
- Equities
- Exchange-traded funds
- Mutual funds
- Real estate investment trusts
- Alternative investments or private equity offerings

## Liquidity

Yellow is my liquid category color. I typically recommend having at least enough yellow money to cover six months of expenses in case of emergency. Yellow assets don't need a lot of growth potential; they just need to be readily available when we need to spend them. The "yellow" category includes assets like:

- Cash
- Checking/savings
- Money market accounts

## Asset Protection

The color of asset protection, to me, is blue. This can incorporate products such as annuities, which we sometimes refer to as one of our Safe Money Strategies. Tranquil, sure — even if it lacks a certain amount of flash. This is the direction I like to see people generally move toward as they're nearing retirement. The green, flashy look of stock market returns and the risk of possible overnight losses are less attractive as we near retirement and look for more consistency and reliability. While this category doesn't come with a lot of liquidity, the products here are backed by an insurance company, a bank, or a government entity. "Blue" products include things such as:

- Certificates of deposit (backed by banks)
- Individual government-based bonds (backed by the U.S. government)
- Life insurance (backed by insurance companies)

- Annuities (backed by insurance companies)

Unfortunately, most of what people think they know about annuities and how they work is either misconstrued, outdated, or just simply false. Consumers owe it to themselves to learn about asset class choices like annuities from an up-to-date, fact-based perspective to evaluate their potential value in a retirement portfolio. We will cover them in more detail in Chapter 8.

# 401(k)s

I want to take a second to specifically address a product many retirees have and will be using to build their retirement income: the 401(k) and other retirement accounts. Any of these retirement accounts (IRAs, 401(k)s, 403(b)s, etc.) are basically "tax wrappers." What do I mean by that? Well, depending on your plan provider, a 401(k) could include target-date funds, passively managed products, stocks, bonds, mutual funds, or even variable, fixed, and fixed index annuities, all collected in one place and governed by rules (a.k.a. the "tax wrapper"). These rules govern how much money you can put inside, what ways you can put it in, when you will pay taxes on it, and when you can take the money out. Inside the 401(k), each of the products inside the "tax wrapper" might have its own fees or commissions in addition to the management fee you pay on the 401(k) itself.

Now, fees can be very misleading. While you can't get something for nothing and fees have traditionally been how many financial companies and professionals make a living, there are new concepts for pricing these days.

I believe there are only three ways to pay for financial products and services:

1. Pay an upfront charge/cost, then pay nothing along the way or when you leave/withdraw.
2. Pay an annual fee, but nothing upfront or when you leave (most clients are familiar with this, and most asset managers do this).
3. Pay nothing upfront or along the way, and if you stay long enough (usually ten years), you can sometimes even pay nothing when you leave.

This last option also often allows for up to 10 percent free withdrawal per contract year, which is more than enough for most people. The third option (most commonly available through annuities and permanent life insurance) also allows the investor access to unique offerings for zero fees! This works for both the client and the financial company, since it is widely accepted that most investment companies only make significant profits from managing client assets for the long term (ten years or more, usually). If the client does not pay anything in this third structure, it may outmatch other fee-based asset manager programs.

So, for those close to retirement, it's important to look at management fees as well as various no-fee options and assess if you think you're getting what you pay for. Over the course of ten years, those costs can add up, and you may have decades ahead of you in which you will need to rely on your assets.

# Dollar-Cost Averaging

With 401(k)s and other market-based retirement products, dollar-cost averaging is a concept that can work in your favor when you are investing for the long term. When the market is trending up, if you are paying in a consistent amount of money, month over month, great; your investments can grow, and you are adding to your assets. When the market takes a dip, no problem; your dollars buy more shares at a lower price. At some point, we hope the market will rebound, in which case your shares can grow and possibly be more valuable than they were before. This concept is what we call "dollar-cost averaging." While it can't ensure a profit or guarantee against losses, it's a time-tested, long-term strategy for investing in a volatile market.

However, when you are in retirement, this strategy may work against you. You may have heard of "reverse" dollar-cost averaging. Before, when the market lost ground, you were "bargain-shopping"; your dollars purchased more assets at a reduced price. When you are in retirement, you are no longer the purchaser; you are selling. So, in a down market, you have to sell more assets to make the same amount of money as what you made in a favorable market. This is what I call a complete paradigm shift.

I've had lots of people meet with me to talk about this, emphasizing how their advisor says, "The market always bounces back, and I have to just hold on for the long term."

There's some basis for this thinking; thus far, the market has always *eventually* rebounded to higher heights than before. But this is no guarantee, and the prospect of potentially higher returns in five years may not be very helpful in retirement if you are relying on the income from those returns to pay this month's electric bill, for example.

It will hardly ever be productive to take money from a losing asset to fund a lifestyle — which is exactly why the blanket "four percent retirement withdrawal rule" is deeply problematic in volatile markets. It's also why we replaced this old, sometimes highly ineffective approach with the updated and more logical paradigm we call "Spend, Protect, Grow."

# Is There a "Perfect" Product?

To bring us back around to the discussion of asset protection, growth, and liquidity, the ideal product would be a "ten" in all three categories, right? Completely guaranteed, doubling in size every few years, and accessible whenever you want. Does such a product exist? Absolutely not.

Instead of running in circles looking for that perfect product, the silver bullet, the unicorn of financial strategies, it's more important to circle back to the concept of a balanced, asset-diverse portfolio.

This is why it could be prudent to work with a knowledgeable financial professional who knows what various financial products can do and how to use them in your personal retirement strategy.* With Spend, Protect, Grow, we can trifurcate assets thoughtfully so that each segment does a specific job for the client.

---

* Investing involves risk, including the potential loss of principal. No investment strategy can guarantee a profit or protect against loss in periods of declining values. Any references to protection benefits or guaranteed/lifetime income streams refer only to fixed insurance products, not securities or investment products. Insurance and annuity product guarantees are backed by the financial strength and claims-paying ability of the issuing insurance company.

# CHAPTER 5

# Retirement Income

Retirement. For many of us, it's what we've saved for and dreamed of, pinning our hopes to a magical someday. Is that someday full of traveling? Is it filled with grandkids? Gardening? Maybe your fondest dream is simply never having to work again, never having to clock in or be accountable to someone else.

Your ability to do these things all hinges on *income*. Without the money to support these dreams, even a basic level of work-free lifestyle is unsustainable. That's why planning for your income in retirement is so foundational. But where do we begin?

It's easy to feel overwhelmed by this question. Some may feel the urge to amass a large lump sum and then try to put it all in one product — insurance, investments, liquid assets — to provide all the growth, liquidity, and income they need. Instead, I think you need a more balanced approach. After all, retirement planning isn't magic. As I mentioned already, there is no single product that can be all things to all people (or even all things to one person). No approach works unilaterally for everyone. That's why it's important to talk to a financial professional who can help you lay down the basics and take you step-by-step through the process. Not only will you have the assurance you have addressed the areas you need to, but you will also have an ally who can help you break down the process and help keep you from feeling overwhelmed.

# Sources of Income

Thinking of all the pieces of your retirement expenses might be intimidating. But, like cleaning out a junk drawer (or, as my very positive-minded mom actually called it, "the everything drawer") or revisiting that garage remodel, once you have laid everything out, you can begin to sort things into categories. Then, with a good overall picture of what your expenses will be, you can start stacking up the resources to cover them.

## Social Security

Social Security is a guaranteed, inflation-adjusted federal insurance program that plays a significant part in many people's retirement plans. From delaying until you've reached full retirement age or beyond to examining spousal benefits, as I discuss elsewhere in this book, there is plenty you can do to try to make the most of this monthly benefit. As with all your retirement income sources, it's important to consider ways to make this resource stretch to provide the most value to you over your lifetime. It is also more relevant than people realize to ascertain how the proper timing of taking Social Security benefits can potentially impact your income tax situation. A comprehensive financial advisor should do this, whereas many brokers or asset managers simply do not.

## Pension

Another generally reliable source of retirement income for you might be a pension if you are one of the lucky people who still has one.

If you don't have a pension, go ahead and skim on to the next section. If you do have a pension, keep on reading.

Because your pension can be such a central piece of your retirement income plan, you will want to put some thought into answering basic questions about it.

How well is your pension funded? Since the heyday of the pension plan, companies and governments have neglected to fund their pension obligations, causing a persistent problem with this otherwise reliable asset.

Consider the factors at play, though. Pensions had been underfunded and gained a boost from strong market performance, most recently in 2021.[23] What happens to the solvency of those pension funds if the market declines?

It can be worthwhile to keep tabs on your pension's health and know what your options are for withdrawing from it. Typically, you have one chance at electing the distribution option at your retirement with no recourse to change at a later date, so you will want to look at all options before making a final decision. If you have already retired and made those decisions, this may be a foregone conclusion. If not, it pays to know what you can expect and what decisions you can make, such as taking spousal options to cover your spouse if they outlive you.

Also, some companies are incentivizing lump-sum payouts of pensions to reduce their balance sheets' projected payment liabilities. If that's the case with your employer, talk to your financial professional to see if it might be prudent to do

---

[23] The Pew Charitable Trusts. November 8, 2023. "Public Retirement Systems Need Sustainable Policies to Navigate Volatile Financial Markets" https://www.pewtrusts.org/en/research-and-analysis/issue-briefs/2023/11/public-retirement-systems-need-sustainable-policies-to-navigate-volatile-financial-markets

something like that or if it might be better to stick with lifetime payments or other options.

## Your 401(k) and IRA

One "modern way" to save for retirement is in a 401(k) or IRA (or their nonprofit or governmental equivalents). These tax-advantaged accounts are, in my opinion, a poor substitute for pensions, but one of the biggest disservices we do to ourselves is not taking full advantage of them in the first place. While the average 401(k) balance for Americans between the ages of forty and forty-nine is $105,500, the median account balance is much lower. The median, which separates half of accounts with higher balances and half with lower balances, is just $34,100.[24] This is deeply concerning to me.

Also, if you have changed jobs over the years, do the work of tracking down any benefits from your past employers. You might have an IRA here or a 401(k) there; keep track of those so you can pull them together and look at those assets when you're ready to look at establishing sources of retirement income. This year, one of my clients, Amy, discovered that at sixty-seven, she had a pension she had forgotten about that should have started paying five years beforehand! The good news is they paid the previous five years out, but it was a windfall she had totally forgotten about.

## Do You Have ...

- Life insurance?
- Annuities?
- Long-term care insurance?
- Any passive income sources?

---

[24] Cheyenne DeVon. CNBC. July 13, 2023. "Here's how much Americans in their 40s have in their 401(k)s"
https://www.cnbc.com/2023/07/13/fidelity-how-much-americans-in-their-40s-have-in-their-401ks.html

- Stock and bond portfolios?
- Liquid assets? (What's in your bank account?)
- Alternative investments?
- Rental properties?

If you are going through the work of sitting with a financial professional, it's important to look at your full retirement income picture and pull together *all* your assets, no matter how big or small. From the free insurance policy offered at your bank to the sizable investment in your brother-in-law's modestly successful furniture store, you want to have a good idea of where your money is.

# Retirement Income Needs

How much income will you need in retirement? How do you determine that? A lot of people work toward a random number, thinking, "If I can just have $2 million, I'll be comfortable in retirement!" Don't get me wrong; it is possible to save up a lot of money and then retire in the hopes you can keep your monthly expenses lower than some set estimation. But I think this carries a general risk of running out of money. Instead, I work with my clients to find out what their current and projected income needs are and then see how we might cover any gaps between what they have and what they want. Also, nowadays, I have noticed that when I ask clients who are about to retire what percentage of their current standard of living they want to fund, they frequently say 100 percent or more! This makes determining sources for funding a substantial and sustainable retirement income more important than ever.

## Goals and Dreams

I like to start with your pie in the sky. Do you find yourself planning for your vacations more thoroughly than you do your retirement? Maybe it's because planning a vacation is less stressful: Having a week at the beach go awry is, well, a walk on the beach compared to running out of money in retirement. Whatever the case, perhaps it would be better if you thought of your retirement as a vacation in and of itself — no clocking in, no boss, no overtime. If you felt unlimited by financial strain, what would you do?

Would an endless vacation for you mean tooling around London, the Greek Islands, and then the Amalfi Coast in Italy? Would it mean mentoring at children's clubs or serving at the local soup kitchen? Or maybe it would mean deepening your ties to those immediately around you — neighbors, friends, and family. Maybe it would mean more time to take part in the hobbies and activities you love — like the pickleball craze currently sweeping the nation! Have you been considering a second (or even third) act as a small-business owner, turning a hobby or passion into a revenue source? Or maybe going back to school or learning to speak a new language?

This is your time to daydream and answer the question: If you could do anything, what would you do?

After that, it's a matter of putting a dollar amount on it. What are the costs of round-the-world travel? One couple I know said their highest priority in retirement was being able to take each of their grandchildren on a cross-country vacation every year. That's a pretty specific goal — one that is reasonably easy to nail down a budget for.

## Current Budget

Compiling a current expense worksheet is one of the trickiest pieces of retirement preparation. Many people assume the expenses of their lives in retirement will be lower. After all, there will be no drive to work, no need for a formal wardrobe, and — perhaps most impactful of all — no more saving for retirement!

Yet, we often underestimate our daily spending habits. That's why I typically ask my clients to send their bank or credit card statements for the past year — they are reflective of your *actual* spending, not just what you think you're spending.

I can't count the number of times I have sat with a couple, asked them about their spending, and heard them throw out a number that seemed incredibly low. When I ask them where the number came from, they usually say they estimated based on their total bills. Yet, our spending is so much more than our mortgage, utilities, cable, phone, car, grocery, or credit card bills.

"What about clothes?" I ask, "Or dining out? What about gifts and coffees and last-minute weekend plans?" That's when the lights come on.

This is why I suggest collecting a year's worth of information. There is usually no such thing as a one-time purchase. Did you buy new furniture? Even if that is a rarity, do you think that will be the last time you *ever* buy furniture? Sadly, my wife reminds me regularly that this should not be the case!

Another hefty expense is spending on the kids. Many of the couples I work with are quick to help their adult children, whether it's something like letting them live in the basement, paying for college, babysitting, paying an occasional bill, or contributing to a grandchild's college fund. Research concluded that 54 percent of those in the Gen Z and millennial age groups lean on parents for financial support. Among those, 23 percent are heavily supported by parents.[25] I may know a little something about this myself!

---

25 Experian. June 27, 2023. "Most Gen Zers and millennials still rely on parents for financial support and feel ashamed asking for help" https://www.experianplc.com/newsroom/press-releases/2023/most-gen-zers-and-millennials-still-rely-on-parents-for-financial-support-and-feel-ashamed-asking-for-help

My clients sometimes protest that what they do for their grown children can stop in retirement. They don't *need* to help. But I get it. Parents like to feel needed. And, while you never want to neglect saving for retirement in favor of taking on financial risks (like your child's student debt), the parents who help their adult children do so in part because it helps them feel fulfilled.

When it comes down to expenses, including (and especially) spending on your family, don't make your initial calculations based on what you *could* whittle your budget down to if you *had* to. Instead, start from where you are. Who wants to live off a bare-bones bank account in retirement?

# Other Expenses

Once you have nailed down your current budget and your dreams or goals for retirement, there are a few other outstanding pieces to think about — some expenses many people don't take the time to consider before making and executing a plan. But I'm assuming you want to get it right, so let's take a look.

## Housing

Do you know where you want to live in retirement? This makes up a substantial piece of your income puzzle — since the typical American household owns a home, and it's generally their largest asset.

Some people prefer to live right where they are for as long as they can. Others have been waiting for retirement to pull the trigger on an ambitious move, like purchasing a new house or even downsizing. Whatever your plans and whatever your reasons, there are quite a few things to consider.

## Mortgage

Do you still have a mortgage? What may have been a nice tax boon in your working years could turn into a financial burden in your retirement. After all, when you are on a limited income, a mortgage is just one more bill sapping your financial strength. It is something to put some thought into whether you plan to age in place or are considering moving to your dream home, buying a house out of state, or living in a retirement community.

## Upkeep and Taxes

A house without a mortgage still requires annual real estate taxes. While it's tempting to think of this as a once-a-year expense, when you have limited earning potential, your annual tax bill might be something into which you should put a little more forethought.

The costs of homeownership aren't just monetary. When you find yourself dealing with more house than you need, it can drain your time and energy. From keeping clutter at bay to keeping the lawn mower running, upkeep can be extensive and expensive. For some, that's a challenge they heartily accept and can comfortably take on. For others, the idea of yard work or cleaning an area larger than they need feels foolish.

## Practicality and Adaptability

Kyle and Jordan are looking to retire within the next two decades. They just sold their old three-bedroom ranch-style house. Their twins are in high school, and the couple has wanted to "upgrade" for years. Now they live in a gorgeous 1940s three-story house with all the kitchen space they ever wanted, five sprawling bedrooms, and a library and media room for themselves and their children. Within months of moving in, the couple realized a house perfect for their active teens would no longer be perfect for them in five to fifteen years.

"We are paying the mortgage for this house, but we've started saving for the next one," said Jordan, "because who wants to climb two flights of stairs to their bedroom when they're seventy-eight?"

Others I know have encountered a similar situation in their personal lives. After a health crisis, one couple found the luxurious tub for two they toiled to install had become a specter of a bad slip and a potential safety risk. It's important to think through what your physical reality could be. I always emphasize to my clients that they should plan for whatever their long-term future might hold, but it's amazing how many people don't give it much thought.

### Contracts and Regulations

If you are looking into a cross-country move, be aware of new tax tables or local ordinances in the area where you are looking to move. After all, you don't want to experience sticker-shock when you are looking at downsizing or reducing your bills in retirement.

Along the same lines, if you are moving into a retirement community, be sure to look at the fine print. What happens if you must move into a different situation for long-term care? Will you be penalized? Will you be responsible for replacing your slot in the community? What are all the fees, and what do they cover?

# Inflation

As I write this in the fall of 2024, America has experienced a wave of inflation following a lengthy period of low inflation. Inflation zoomed to 9.1 percent in June 2022, its highest mark since November 1981.[26] By the end of 2023, the inflation rate decreased to 3.1 percent.[27]

Core inflation is yet another measurement that excludes goods with prices that tend to be more volatile, such as food and energy costs. Core inflation for a twelve-month period ending in November 2023 was 4.0 percent. It so happened that energy prices decreased 5.4 percent over that timeframe.[28]

However, inflation isn't a one-time bump; it has a cumulative effect that can impact the price of groceries more than other goods. Even with relatively low inflation over the past few decades, an item you bought in 1997 for $2 will cost about $3.89 today.[29] Want to go to a show? A $20 ticket in 1997 would cost $45.12 in 2024.[30]

What if we hit a stretch in retirement like the late seventies and early eighties, when annual inflation rates of 10 percent became the norm? It may be wise to consider some extra padding in your retirement income plan to account for any potential increase in inflation in the future.

---

[26] Trading Economics. 2024. "United States Inflation Rate" https://tradingeconomics.com/united-states/inflation-cpi

[27] Statista. April 15, 2024. "Monthly 12-month inflation rate in the United States from March 2020 to March 2024" https://www.statista.com/statistics/273418/unadjusted-monthly-inflation-rate-in-the-us

[28] U.S. Inflation Calculator. 2024. "United States Core Inflation Rates (1957-2024)" https://www.usinflationcalculator.com/inflation/united-states-core-inflation-rates/

[29] in2013dollars.com. 2024. "$2 in 1997 is worth $3.89 today" https://www.in2013dollars.com/us/inflation/1997?amount=2

[30] in2013dollars.com. 2024. "Admission to movies, theaters, and concerts priced at $20 in 1997 ->$45.12 in 2024" https://www.in2013dollars.com/Admission-to-movies,-theaters,-and-concerts/price-inflation

# Shrinkflation

Another important yet often overlooked factor to consider is called "shrinkflation." Essentially a form of hidden inflation, shrinkflation signifies a reduction in packaging while retaining a similar price as before.

For example, as you walk down a grocery store aisle, you spot your favorite pickles. The jar still costs the same — roughly $5 — and you add it to your cart. Then you get home, and the container seems different after digging out a few crispy dills. You examine the jar and discover it contains fewer ounces than previous jars you purchased. However, you paid roughly the same price for your pickles.

Now, move over to the aisle featuring salty snacks. You might notice a sale on a certain brand of chips, though you must buy three or four bags to receive a discount promoted by the store. You decide to purchase that many bags to capitalize on the lower price. When you get home, you notice the packaging is more air than you anticipated. The deal you accepted may not have been as thrifty as you perceived.

Shrinkflation can be a way for companies to quietly boost or retain profit margins without having to change much else — essentially, they are simply charging the same price for less product. I still remember a world-renowned hamburger chain reducing the size of their bun some years ago to make their burgers seem bigger. Companies do this because customers are more likely to spot price increases than size reductions. However, research has also shown that these shrinkflation tactics can backfire into negative consumer perceptions of their brands once they come to light. Who wants to pay the same for less, especially when they have already grown accustomed to getting more for their money's worth?[31]

# Aging

Also, in the expense category, think about longevity, as we discussed in Chapter 1. We all hope to age gracefully. However, it's important to face the prospect of aging with a sense of realism.

For many families, the elephant in the room is long-term care. No one wants to admit they will likely need it, but estimates indicate almost 70 percent of us will.[32] Aging is a significant piece of retirement income planning because you'll want to figure out how to set aside money for your care, either at home or away from it. The more comfortable you get with discussing your wishes and plans with your loved ones, the easier planning for the financial side of it can be.

I denote health care and potential long-term care costs in more detail earlier in Chapter 2 of this book, but suffice it to say nursing home care tends to be very expensive and typically isn't something you get to choose when you will need.

It isn't just the costs of long-term care that pose a concern in living longer. It's also about covering the possible costs of everything else associated with living longer. For instance, if Parnell retires from his job as a biochemical engineer at age sixty-five, perhaps he plans to have a very decent income for twenty years until he turns eighty-five. But what if he lives until

[31] Daniel Liberto. Investopedia. November 16, 2023. "Shrinkflation: What It Is, Reasons for It, How to Spot It"
https://www.investopedia.com/terms/s/shrinkflation.asp
[32] Moll Law Group. 2024. "The Cost of Long-Term Care"
https://www.molllawgroup.com/the-cost-of-long-term-care.html

he's ninety-five? That's a whole third — ten years — more of personal income he will need.

# Putting It All Together

Whew! So, you have pulled together what you have, and you have a pretty good idea of where you want to be. Now, you and your financial professional can go about the work of arranging what assets you *have* to cover what you *need* — and how you might try to cover any gaps.

Like the proverbial man in the Bible who built his house on a rock[33], I like to help my clients figure out how to cover their day-to-day living expenses — their needs — with protected assets and other guaranteed income sources like pensions and Social Security.

Again, you should keep in mind there isn't one single financial vehicle, asset, or source to fill all your needs, and that's okay. One of the challenges of planning for your income in retirement concerns figuring out what products and strategies to use. You can release some of that stress when you accept the fact you will probably need a diverse portfolio — potentially with bonds, stocks, insurance, annuities, mutual funds, ETFs, and other income sources — not just one massive money pile.

One way to help shore up your income gaps is by working with your financial professional and a qualified tax advisor to help mitigate your tax exposure. If you have a 401(k) or IRA, a tax advisor in your corner may be able to help you figure out how and when to take distributions from your account in a way that doesn't push you into a higher tax bracket. In my experience, however, most people's "accountants" don't focus on tax planning like a comprehensive financial advisor might.

---

[33] Matthew 7:24-27 (New International Version)

Effective tax planning isn't necessarily about "adding" to your income. Especially regarding retirement, it's less about what you make than it is about what you keep. Paying a lower tax bill keeps more money in your pocket, which is where you want it when it comes to retirement income.

Most clients seem overly concerned with the taxes they might pay during the current year or the one immediately prior. However, for those looking to make a significant difference in keeping what they make, it is much more important to play the long game and plan to save the most they can over a lifetime. This often involves paying a little bit more for a few years in order to pay considerably less in the long run. A good advisor can help you consider strategies in the present that can enable such a phenomenon in the future.

Now you can look at ways to cover your remaining retirement goals. Are there products like long-term care insurance specific to a certain kind of expense you anticipate? Is there a particular asset you want to use for your "play" money — money for trips and gifts for the grandkids? Is there any way you can portion off money for those charitable legacy plans?

Once you have analyzed your income wants, needs, and the assets necessary to realistically cover them, you may have a gap. The masterstroke of a competent financial professional will be to help you figure out how you will cover that gap. Will you need to cut out a round of golf a week? Maybe skip the new car? Or will you need to take more substantial action?

One way to cover an income gap is to consider working longer or even part-time before retirement and even after that magical calendar date. This may not be the best "plan" for you; disabilities, work demands, and physical or emotional limitations can hinder the best-laid plans to continue working. However, if it is physically possible for you, this is one considerable way to help your assets last for more than one reason.

In fact, 55 percent of Americans responding to a survey report they plan to work part-time after retiring, while 15 percent expect compensation from work to be their primary source of retirement income.[34]

When you're retired, you no longer have an employer paying you a steady check. It is up to you to make sure you have saved and planned for the income you need.

---

[34] Kerry Hannon. Yahoo! Finance. July 15, 2023. "Future retirees plan to work longer, partly due to savings shortfalls"
https://finance.yahoo.com/news/future-retirees-plan-to-work-longer-partly-due-to-savings-shortfalls-160038419.html

# CHAPTER 6

# Social Security

S ocial Security is often the foundation of retirement income. Backed by the strength of the U.S. Treasury, it provides perhaps the most dependable paycheck you will have in retirement.

From the time you collect your first paycheck from the job that made you a bona fide taxpayer, you are paying into the grand old Social Security system. What grew and developed out of the pressures of the Great Depression has become one of the most popular government programs in the country, and if you pay in for the equivalent of ten years or more, you, too, can benefit from the Social Security program.

Now, before we get into the nitty-gritty of Social Security, I'd like to address a current concern: Will Social Security still be there for you when you reach retirement age?

## The Future of Social Security

This question is ever-present as headlines trumpet an underfunded Social Security program alongside the sea of baby boomers retiring in droves and the comparatively smaller pool of younger people who are funding the system.

The Social Security Administration itself acknowledges this concern as each Social Security statement now contains a link to its website (ssa.gov) and a page entitled, "Will Social Security Be There For Me?"

Just a reminder, as if you needed one, that nothing in life is guaranteed. Additionally, depending on who you're listening to, Social Security funds may run low before 2034, thanks to the financial instability and government spending that accompanied the 2020 COVID-19 pandemic.

Before you get too discouraged, though, here are a few thoughts to keep you going:

- Even if the program is only paying 75 to 78 cents on the dollar for scheduled benefits, this is notably not zero.
- The Social Security Administration has made changes in the distant and near past to help protect the fund's solvency, including increasing retirement ages and striking certain filing strategies.
- There are many changes Congress could make, and lawmakers routinely discuss ideas for amending the system, such as further increasing full retirement age and eligibility.
- One thing no one is seriously discussing? Reneging on current obligations to retirees or the soon-to-retire.

Take heart. The real answer to the question, "Will Social Security be there for me?" is still yes. It may continue to change, but it remains an American mainstay.

This question is important to consider when you look at how much we, as a nation, rely on this program. Did you know Social

Security benefits replace about 37 percent of a person's original income when they retire?[35]

If you ask me, that's a pretty significant piece of your retirement income puzzle.

Another caveat? You may not realize this, but no one can legally "advise" you about your Social Security benefits.

"But, Phil," you may be thinking, "isn't that part of what you do? And what about that nice gentleman at the Social Security Administration office I spoke with on the phone?"

Don't get me wrong. Social Security Administration employees know their stuff. They are trained to understand policies and programs, and they are usually pretty quick to tell you what you can and cannot do. But the government specifically stipulates that because Social Security is a benefit you alone have paid into and earned, your Social Security decisions are *also* yours alone.

When it comes to financial professionals, we can't push you in any direction, but — there's a big but here — working with a well-informed financial professional is still incredibly handy for your Social Security decisions. Why? Because someone who's worth their salt will know what withdrawal strategies might pertain to your specific situation and will ask questions that can help you determine what you are looking for when it comes to your Social Security.

For instance, some people want the highest possible monthly benefit. Others want to start their benefits early, and not always because of financial need. I heard about one man who called in

---

[35] Center on Budget and Policy Priorities. April 17, 2023. "Top Ten Facts About Social Security"
https://www.cbpp.org/sites/default/files/atoms/files/8-8-16socsec.pdf

to start his Social Security payments the day he qualified just because he liked to think of it as the government paying back a debt it owed him, and he enjoyed the feeling of receiving a check from Uncle Sam.

Whatever your reasons, questions, or feelings regarding Social Security, the decision is yours alone, but working with a financial professional can help you put your options in perspective by showing you — both with industry knowledge and with proprietary software or planning processes — where your benefits fit into your overall strategy for retirement income.

# Full Retirement Age

When it comes to Social Security, it seems like many people only think so far as "yes." They don't take the time to understand the various options available. Instead, because it is common knowledge you can begin your benefits at age sixty-two, that's what some of us do. While more people are opting to delay taking benefits, age sixty-two is still a popular age to start.[36]

Some people fail to understand that starting benefits early may leave significant money on the table. You see, the Social Security Administration bases your monthly benefit on two factors: your earnings history and your full retirement age (FRA).

From your earnings history, the SSA pulls the thirty-five years you made the most money and uses a mathematical indexing formula to figure out a monthly average from those years. If you

---

[36] Emily Brandon and Erica Sandberg. U.S. News & World Report. August 14, 2023. "The Most Popular Ages to Collect Social Security" https://money.usnews.com/money/retirement/social-security/articles/the-most-popular-ages-to-collect-social-security

paid into the system for less than thirty-five years, then every year you didn't pay in will be counted as a zero.

Once they have calculated what your monthly earnings would be at FRA, the government then calculates what to put on your check based on how close you are to FRA. FRA was originally set at sixty-five, but as the population aged and lifespans lengthened, the government shifted FRA later and later, based on an individual's year of birth. Check out the following chart to see when you will reach FRA.[37]

[37] Social Security Administration. 2024. "Starting Your Retirement Benefits Early"
https://www.ssa.gov/benefits/retirement/planner/agereduction.html

| Age to Receive Full Social Security Benefits* | |
|---|---|
| *(Called "full retirement age" [FRA] or "normal retirement age.")* | |
| Year of Birth* | FRA |
| 1937 or earlier | 65 |
| 1938 | 65 and 2 months |
| 1939 | 65 and 4 months |
| 1940 | 65 and 6 months |
| 1941 | 65 and 8 months |
| 1942 | 65 and 10 months |
| 1943-1954 | 66 |
| 1955 | 66 and 2 months |
| 1956 | 66 and 4 months |
| 1957 | 66 and 6 months |
| 1958 | 66 and 8 months |
| 1959 | 66 and 10 months |
| 1960 and later | 67 |
| *\*If you were born on January 1 of any year, you should refer to the previous year. (If you were born on the 1st of the month, we figure your benefit [and your full retirement age] as if your birthday was in the previous month.)*[38] | |

When you reach FRA, you are eligible to receive 100 percent of whatever the Social Security Administration calculates as your full monthly benefit.

---

[38] Social Security Administration. 2024. "Normal Retirement Age" https://www.ssa.gov/oact/progdata/nra.html

Starting at age sixty-two, for every year before FRA you claim benefits, your monthly check is reduced by 5 percent or more. Conversely, for every year you delay taking benefits past FRA, your monthly benefit increases by 8 percent (until age seventy — after that, there is no monetary advantage to delaying Social Security benefits). While your circumstances and needs may vary, a lot of financial professionals still urge people to at least consider delaying until they reach age seventy.

Why wait?[39]

| Taking benefits early could affect your monthly check by _____. | | | | | | | | |
|---|---|---|---|---|---|---|---|---|
| 62 | 63 | 64 | 65 | 66 | FRA 67 | 68 | 69 | 70 |
| -30% | -25% | -20% | -13.3% | -6.7% | 0 | +8% | +16% | +24% |

[40]

## My Social Security

If you are over thirty, you have probably received a notice from the Social Security Administration telling you to activate something called "My Social Security." This is a handy way to learn more about your particular benefit options, keep track of your earnings record, and calculate the benefits you have accrued over the years.

Essentially, My Social Security is an online account you can activate to see your personal Social Security picture. You can access this information at www.ssa.gov/myaccount. This can be extremely helpful when it comes to planning for income in

---

[39] Social Security Administration. 2024. "Retirement Benefits" https://www.ssa.gov/pubs/EN-05-10035.pdf
[40] Social Security Administration. 2024. "Effect of Early or Delayed Retirement on Retirement Benefits" https://www.ssa.gov/oact/ProgData/ar_drc.html

retirement and figuring out the difference between your anticipated income versus anticipated expenses.

## Cost-of-Living Adjustment (COLA)

Social Security is a largely guaranteed piece of the retirement puzzle: If you get a statement that reads you should expect $1,000 a month, you can be sure you will receive $1,000 a month. But there is one variable detail, and that is something called the cost-of-living adjustment.

The COLA is an increase in your monthly check meant to address inflation in everyday life. After all, your expenses will likely continue to experience inflation in retirement, but you will no longer have the opportunity for raises, bonuses, or promotions you had when you were working. Instead, Social Security receives an annual cost-of-living increase tied to the Department of Labor's Consumer Price Index for Urban Wage Earners and Clerical Workers (CPI-W). If the CPI-W measurement shows inflation rose a certain amount for regular goods and services, then Social Security recipients will see that reflected in their COLA.

COLA adjustments have climbed as high as 14.3 percent (1980), and in 2023, they reached 8.7 percent — the largest increase in more than forty years. In a no- or low-inflation environment (such as in 2010, 2011, and 2016), Social Security recipients will not receive an adjustment.[41] The 2024 adjustment decreased to 3.2 percent.[42] Some view the COLA as a perk, bump, or bonus, but in reality, it works more like this: Your mom sends you to the store with $3.50 for a gallon of milk. Milk costs exactly $3.50. The next week, you go back with that same amount, but it is now $3.60 for a gallon, so you go back to Mom, and she

[41] Social Security Administration. 2024. "Cost-Of-Living Adjustments" https://www.ssa.gov/oact/cola/colaseries.html
[42] Social Security Administration. 2024. "Cost-of-Living Adjustment (COLA) Information for 2024" https://www.ssa.gov/cola/

gives you 10 cents. You aren't bringing home more milk — it just costs more money.

The COLA is less about "making more money" and more about keeping seniors' purchasing power from eroding when inflation is a big factor. Still, don't let that detract from your enthusiasm about COLAs. After all, what if Mom's solution was: "Here's the same $3.50. Try to find a dime from somewhere else to get that milk!"?

# Spousal Benefits

We've talked about FRA, but another big Social Security decision involves spousal benefits.

If you or your spouse has a long stretch of zeros in your earnings history — perhaps if one of you stayed home for years, caring for children or sick relatives — you may want to consider filing for spousal benefits instead of filing on your own earnings history. A spousal benefit can be up to 50 percent of the primary wage earner's benefit at full retirement age.

To begin drawing a spousal benefit, you must be at least sixty-two years old, and the primary wage earner must have already filed for their benefit. While there are penalties for taking spousal benefits early, you cannot earn credits for delaying past full retirement age.[43]

As I wrote, the spousal benefit can be a big deal for those who don't have a very long pay history, but it's important to weigh your own earned benefits against the option of withdrawing based on a fraction of your spouse's benefits.

---

[43] Social Security Administration. 2024. "Benefits For Your Family" https://www.ssa.gov/benefits/retirement/planner/applying7.html

To look at how this could play out, let's use a hypothetical couple: Ted, who is sixty, and Donna, who is sixty-two.

Let's say Donna's benefit at FRA — in her case, sixty-seven — would be $3,200. If Donna begins her benefits right now (five years before FRA), her monthly check will be $2,240. If Ted begins taking spousal benefits in two years at the earliest date possible, his monthly benefits will be reduced to $1,120 per month.

What if Donna and Ted both wait until FRA? At sixty-seven, Donna begins taking her full benefit of $3,200 a month. Two years later, when he reaches age sixty-seven, Ted will qualify for $1,600 a month (half of Donna's FRA benefit). By waiting until FRA, the couple's monthly benefit goes from $3,360 to $4,800.

What if Donna delays until age seventy to get her maximum possible benefit? For each year past FRA she delays, her monthly benefits increase by 8 percent. This means that at seventy, she could file for a monthly benefit of $3,968. However, delayed retirement credits do not affect spousal benefits, so as soon as Donna files at seventy, Ted would also file (at age sixty-eight) for his maximum benefit of $1,600, so their highest possible combined monthly check is $5,568.[44]

When it comes to your Social Security benefits, you obviously will want to consider whether a monthly check based on a fraction of your spouse's earnings will be comparable to or larger than your own earnings history.

## Divorced Spouses

There are a few considerations for those among us who have gone through a divorce. If you 1) were married for ten years or

44 Social Security Administration. 2024. "Social Security Benefits"
https://www.ssa.gov/OACT/quickcalc/spouse.html#calculator

more *and* 2) have since been divorced for at least two years *and* 3) are unmarried *and* 4) your ex-spouse qualifies to begin Social Security, you qualify for a spousal benefit based on your ex-spouse's earnings history at FRA. A divorced spousal benefit is different from the married spousal benefit in one way: You don't have to wait for your ex-spouse to file before you can file yourself.[45]

For instance, Rick and Tammy were married for fifteen years before their divorce, when he was thirty-six and she was forty. Tammy has been remarried for twenty years, and although Rick briefly remarried, his second marriage ended after a few years. Rick's benefits are largely calculated based on his many years of volunteering in schools, meaning his personal monthly benefit is close to zero.

Although Tammy has deferred her retirement (opting to delay benefits until she is seventy), Rick can begin taking benefits calculated from Tammy's work history at FRA as early as sixty-two. However, he will also have the option of waiting until FRA to collect the maximum or 50 percent of Tammy's earned monthly benefit at her FRA.

## Widowed Spouses

If your marriage ended with the death of your spouse, you might claim a benefit for your spouse's earned income as their widow/widower called a survivor's benefit. Unlike spousal benefits or divorced benefits, if your spouse dies, you can claim their full benefit. Also, unlike spousal benefits, you can begin taking income when you turn sixty if you need to. However, as with other benefit options, your monthly check will be permanently reduced for withdrawing benefits before FRA.

---

[45] Social Security Administration. 2024. "Benefits For Your Family" https://www.ssa.gov/benefits/retirement/planner/applying7.html

If your spouse began taking benefits before they died, you can't delay withdrawing your survivor's benefits to get delayed credits. The Social Security Administration maintains you can only get as much from a survivor's benefit as your deceased spouse might have received had they lived.[46]

# Taxes, Taxes, Taxes

With Social Security — as with everything — it is important to consider taxes. It may be surprising, but your Social Security benefits are not tax-free. Despite having been taxed to accrue those benefits in the first place, you may have to pay Uncle Sam income taxes on up to 85 percent of your Social Security.

The Social Security Administration figures these taxes using what they call "the provisional income formula." Your provisional income formula differs from the adjusted gross income you use for your regular income taxes. Instead, to find out how much of your Social Security benefit is taxable, the Social Security Administration calculates it this way:

*Provisional Income = Adjusted Gross Income + Nontaxable Interest + ½ of Social Security*

See that piece about nontaxable interest? That generally means interest from tax-free government bonds and notes. It surprises many people that although you may not pay taxes on those assets, their income will count against you when it comes to Social Security taxation.

---

[46] Social Security Administration. 2024. "Receiving Survivors Benefits Early" https://www.ssa.gov/planners/survivors/survivorchartred.html

Once you have figured out your provisional income (also called "combined income"), you can use the following chart to figure out your Social Security taxes.[47]

| Taxes on Social Security | | |
|---|---|---|
| *Provisional Income = Adjusted Gross Income + Nontaxable Interest + ½ of Social Security* | | |
| If you are ____ and your provisional income is____, then ... | | Uncle Sam will tax ___ of your Social Security. |
| Single | Married, filing jointly | |
| Less than $25,000 | Less than $32,000 | 0% |
| $25,000 to $34,000 | $32,000 to $44,000 | Up to 50% |
| More than $34,000 | More than $44,000 | Up to 85% |

[48]

This is one more reason why working with financial and tax professionals may benefit you. They can help you look at your entire financial picture to make your overall retirement plan as tax-efficient as possible — including your Social Security benefit.

For many of our clients retiring before or even at FRA, the question looms about whether it would make more sense to take their benefit then or suspend them until up to age seventy. With assumptions about their life expectancy agreed upon for planning purposes, we help them determine which age makes the most sense.

---

47 Julia Kagan. Investopedia. October 8, 2022. "Provisional Taxes: What They are and how They Work"
https://www.investopedia.com/terms/p/provisional-income.asp
48 Ibid.

Part of this calculation (for which use professional-grade software) depends on other assets they may be able to draw from while they wait to collect. We also consider distributing pre-tax assets immediately or even taking Roth conversions for several years before raising their taxable income due to Social Security. We gave this process of determining which assets to draw from and when a name: *strategic distribution planning*.

While we cover SDP in other places in this book, we define it as "the thoughtful arrangement of distributions from assets, whether pre-tax or after-tax, at a cadence which enables one to not only fund the standard of living they want in retirement but also pay the least in total income taxes for the rest of their lives." Aligning resources (including Social Security) for the most tax-efficient distribution over a lifetime is a common request from clients who hire us to do their comprehensive financial planning.

# Working and Social Security: The Earnings Test

If you haven't reached FRA but you started your Social Security benefits and are still working, things get a little hairy.

Because you have started Social Security payments, the Social Security Administration will pay out your benefits (at that reduced rate, of course, because you haven't reached your FRA). Yet, because you are working, the organization must also withhold from your check to add to your benefits, which you are already collecting. See how this complicates matters?

To address the situation, the government has what is called the earnings test. For 2024, you can earn up to $22,320 without it affecting your Social Security check if you're younger than full retirement age. But, for every $2 you earn past that amount, the

Social Security Administration will withhold $1. The earnings test loosens in the year of your FRA; if you are reaching FRA in 2024, you can earn up to $59,520 before you run into the earnings test, and the government only withholds $1 for every $3 past that amount.

The month you reach FRA, you are no longer subject to any earnings withholding. For instance, if you are still working and will turn sixty-seven on December 28, 2024, you would only have to worry about the earnings test until December, and then you can ignore it entirely. Keep in mind, the money the government withholds from your Social Security benefits while you are working before FRA will be tacked back onto your benefits check after FRA.[49]

# Railroad Retirement Benefits

The Railroad Retirement Act was established in 1934 to address concerns about existing pension programs' ability to provide former railroad employees with old-age benefits.[50] The Act continues to provide benefits to retired and disabled workers and their dependents based on their length of employment in the industry. Although there are similarities to Social Security, there are considerable differences, which include payment amounts, eligibility age, and taxation obligations.

Like Social Security, Railroad Retirement Benefits (RRB) are funded from payroll taxes of current employees and employers. Also, both types of benefits are received by retirees as a monthly check. RRBs use the same formula to calculate COLAs as Social Security.

---

[49] Social Security Administration. 2024. "Receiving Benefits While Working"
https://www.ssa.gov/benefits/retirement/planner/whileworking.html
[50] U.S. Railroad Retirement Board. January 2024. "Agency Overview"
https://www.rrb.gov/OurAgency/AgencyOverview

The differences between the two retirement programs are intricate. The average monthly RRB payment is more generous than Social Security because railroad workers pay higher taxes into the program. Another major difference is the age at which railroad workers are eligible to begin collecting benefits: A railroad worker with thirty or more years of service is eligible for full benefits at age sixty without a reduction.

The taxation of RRBs is more complex than Social Security payments. To determine the tax, RRBs are broken down into two components:

- Tier I benefits resemble Social Security, a private pension, or a combination of both
- Tier II benefits are similar to a private pension[51]

The portion of the Tier I benefit equivalent to Social Security is taxed the same way as Social Security benefits, but the portion not equivalent is fully taxable. Regarding the Tier II, a portion is always taxable and subject to ordinary income tax rates.[52]

---

[51] Kurt Woock. NerdWallet. February 7, 2024. "Railroad Retirement Board: What It Is, How It Works"
https://www.nerdwallet.com/article/investing/social-security/what-is-the-railroad-retirement-board
[52] True Tamplin. Finance Strategists. September 7, 2023. "Is Railroad Retirement Income Taxable?"
https://www.financestrategists.com/retirement-planning/retirement-income-planning/is-railroad-retirement-income-taxable/

# CHAPTER 7

# 401(k)s, IRAs, and Roth IRAs

H ave you heard? Today's retirement is not your parents' retirement. You see, back in the day, it was pretty common to work for one company for the vast majority of your career and then retire with a gold watch and a pension.

The gold watch was a symbol of the quality time you had put in at that company, but the pension was more than a symbol. Instead, it was a guarantee — as solid as your employer — that they would repay your hard work with a certain amount of income in your old age. In many ways, this was a fair trade for those who committed their careers to a single company for a lifetime income. But do you see the caveat there? Your pension's guarantee was *as solid as your employer*. The problem was, what if your employer went under?

Companies that failed couldn't pay their retired employees' pensions, leading to financial challenges for many. Beginning in 1974 with Congress' passage of the Employee Retirement Income Security Act, federal legislation and regulations aimed at protecting retirees were everywhere. One piece of legislation included a relatively obscure section of the Internal Revenue Code, added in 1978 — Section 401(k), to be specific.

IRC section 401, subsection k, created tax advantages for employer-sponsored financial products, even if the main contributors were the employees themselves. Over the years, more employers took note, beginning an age of transition away from pensions and toward 401(k) plans. A 401(k) is a retirement account with certain tax benefits and restrictions on investments or other financial products inside of it.

Essentially, 401(k)s and their individual retirement account (IRA) counterparts are "wrappers" that provide tax benefits around assets; typically, the assets that compose IRAs and 401(k)s are mutual funds, stock and bond mixes, and money market accounts. However, IRA and 401(k) contents are becoming more diverse these days, with some companies offering different kinds of annuity options within their plans.

Today, there is also a preponderance of singular mutual funds designed to align with the typical risk tolerance of folks who expect to retire in a certain year, based upon an assumed age of, say, sixty-five. These target-date funds (sometimes referred to as default funds) are for people who feel ill prepared to make their own mutual fund or investment selections. While they appear to be a sensible approach to helping the overwhelmed or underinformed, they are a distant second choice to a professional asset class allocation prepared by a qualified financial advisor.

There are two reasons for this perspective. First, target date funds imply that all people of a certain age would want the exact same investment mix — which would be like assuming all sixty-five-year-olds buy the same cars, live in the same houses, have the same hobbies, go on the same vacations, etc. Second, it is hard for most laypersons who choose these target date funds to determine exactly what is in them and how they will be expected to change over time. For these reasons, given the option, most financial advisors will likely dismantle these allocations in favor of known investments and a tolerance for risk tailored to their clients' preferences and lifestyles.

Where pensions are defined-*benefit* plans, 401(k)s and IRAs are defined-*contribution* plans. The one-word change outlines the basic difference. Pensions spell out what you can expect to receive from the plan but not necessarily how much money it will take to fund those benefits. With 401(k)s, an employer sets a standard for how much they will contribute (if any), and you can be certain of what you are contributing. Still, there is no outline of what you can expect to receive in return for those contributions.

Modern employment looks very different. A 2022 survey by the Bureau of Labor Statistics determined U.S. workers stayed with their employers for a median of 4.1 years. Workers aged fifty-five to sixty-four had a little more staying power and were most likely to stay with their employer for about ten years.[53] Participation in 401(k) plans appears solid. In a study it conducted, Vanguard reported a record plan participation rate of 83 percent in 2022. Plans with automatic enrollment drew a 93 percent participation rate.[54]

Those statistics make it clear that 401(k) plans have replaced pensions at many companies and, for that matter, the now-proverbial gold watch.

If there is anything to learn from this paradigm shift, it's that you must look out for yourself. Whether you have worked for a company for two years or twenty, you are still the one who has to look out for your own best interests. That holds doubly true

[53] U.S. Bureau of Labor Statistics. September 22, 2022. "Employee Tenure Summary" https://www.bls.gov/news.release/tenure.nr0.htm
[54] Vanguard. 2023. "How America Saves 2023" https://institutional.vanguard.com/content/dam/inst/iig-transformation/has/2023/pdf/has-insights/how-america-saves-report-2023.pdf

when it comes to preparing for retirement. If you are one of the lucky ones who still has a pension, good for you. But for the rest of us, it is likely a 401(k) — or possibly one of its nonprofit- or government-sector counterparts, a 403(b) or 457 plan — is one of your biggest assets for retirement.

Some employers offer incentives to contribute to their company plans, like a company match. On that subject, I have one thing to say: *Do it!* Nothing in life is free, as they say, but a company match on your retirement funds is about as close to free money as it gets. If you can contribute the minimum to qualify for your company's match at all, go for it.

Now, it's likely that during our working years, we mostly "set and forget" our 401(k) funding. Because it is tax-advantaged, your employer is taking money from your paycheck — before taxes — and putting it into your plan for you. Maybe you were able to pick a selection of investments, or maybe your company only offers one choice of investment in your 401(k). Either way, while you are gainfully employed, your most impactful decision may just be the decision to continue funding your plan in the first place. But when you are ready to retire or move jobs, you have choices to make requiring a little more thought and care.

When you are ready to part ways with your job, you have a few options:

- Leave the money where it is
- Take the cash (and pay income taxes and perhaps a 10 percent additional federal tax if you are younger than age fifty-nine-and-one-half)
- Transfer the money to another employer plan (if the new plan allows)
- Roll the money over into a self-directed IRA

Today, most of these 401(k) plans now also offer what is called In-Service Transfer (IST) provisions, where you can roll over your balances to an IRA as soon as you reach age fifty-nine-and-a-half with no income tax consequences while still working at your company. This can be a very useful provision to consolidate your assets into one place for ease of management and will undoubtedly offer considerably more investment options than the limited selections chosen by your employer's plan. You can also continue contributing to the 401(k) even after transferring your existing balance. Consult your Retirement Plan Summary (sometimes called a Summary Plan Document) to determine if it covers such provisions.

Now, these are just general options. You will have to decide — hopefully with the help of a financial professional — what's right for you. For instance, 401(k)s are typically pretty closely tied to the companies offering them, so when changing jobs, it may not always be possible to transfer a 401(k) to another 401(k). Leaving the money where it is may also be out of the question — some companies have direct cash payout or rollover policies once someone is no longer employed.

Also, remember what we mentioned earlier about how we change jobs more often these days? That means you likely have a 401(k) with your current company, but you may also have a string of retirement accounts trailing you from other jobs. For many of our clients, self-directing these assets in an IRA Rollover seems simpler and easier to manage — not to mention that in an IRA, you can typically choose from over 18,000 investment choices, whereas in your old company's 401(k), you might have had forty to sixty choices if you were lucky. I sometimes help people understand this by asking if their favorite sports team were to play an All-Star Team comprised of the best players in the entire league, who would likely win? It's a rhetorical question — the All-Star Team would likely win most of the time. This analogy applies to an IRA having access to more and better "players" than a single 401(k). Having someone knowledgeable on your side to guide you through these kinds of decisions is another reason why it's good to have a financial professional help you choose the investments.

When it comes to your retirement income, it's important to be able to pull together *all* your assets so you can examine what you have and where, and then decide what you will do with it.

## Tax-Qualified, Tax-Preferred, Tax-Deferred ... Still TAXED

Financial media often cite IRAs and 401(k)s for their tax benefits. After all, with traditional plans, you put your money in pre-tax, and it hopefully grows for years — even decades — untaxed. That's why these accounts are called "tax-qualified" or "tax-deferred" assets. They aren't *tax-free!* Rarely does Uncle Sam allow business to continue without receiving his piece of the pie, and your retirement assets are no different. If you didn't pay taxes on the front end, you will pay taxes on the money you withdraw from these accounts in retirement. Don't get me wrong: This isn't an inherently good or bad thing; it's just the way it is. It's important to understand, though, for the sake of planning ahead.

In retirement, many people assume they will be in a lower tax bracket. As referenced in the Taxes chapter, for retirees with healthy balances in tax-deferred assets, their retirement marginal tax rate may be the same or even more than their pre-retirement rate. The timing involved with beginning Social Security or in shifting or converting funds out of tax-deferred assets is of strategic concern because of taxes owed on those assets.

Keep in mind, IRAs, 401(k)s, and their alternatives have a few limitations because of their special tax status. For one thing, the IRS sets limits on your contributions to these retirement accounts. If you are contributing to a 401(k) or an equivalent nonprofit or government plan, your annual contribution limit is $23,000 (as of 2024). If you are fifty or older, the IRS allows additional contributions, called "catch-up contributions," of up to $7,500 on top of the regular limit of $23,000. For an IRA, the limit is $7,000, with a catch-up limit of an additional $1,000.[55] Beginning in 2026, catch-up contributions for individuals with income exceeding $145,000 must be transferred into a Roth IRA.[56]

Because their tax advantages come from their intended use as retirement income, withdrawing funds from these accounts before you turn fifty-nine-and-one-half can carry stiff penalties. In addition to fees your investment management company might charge, you will have to pay income tax *and* a 10 percent federal tax penalty, with a few exceptions.

The fifty-nine-and-one-half rule for retirement accounts is incredibly important to remember, especially when you're young. Younger workers are often tempted to cash out an IRA from a previous employer and then are surprised to find their checks missing 20 percent of the account value to income taxes, penalty taxes, and account fees.

Many millennials say that while they may be socking money away in their workplace retirement plan, it is often the *only* place they are saving. This could be problematic later because of the fifty-nine-and-one-half rule; what if you have an emergency? It is important to fund your retirement, but you need to have some liquid assets handy as emergency funds. This

[55] Fidelity. March 4, 2024. "IRA contribution limits for 2023 and 2024" https://www.fidelity.com/learning-center/smart-money/ira-contribution-limits
[56] Robert Powell. The Street. September 11, 2023. "Ask the Hammer: Catch-up Contributions Now Permitted Until 2026" https://www.thestreet.com/retirement-daily/ask-the-hammer/catch-up-contributions-now-permitted-until-2026

can help you avoid breaking into your retirement accounts and incurring taxes and penalties because of the fifty-nine-and-one-half rule.

# Required Minimum Distributions (RMDs)

Remember how we talked about the 401(k) or IRA being a "tax wrapper" for your funds? Well, eventually, Uncle Sam will want a bite of that candy bar. So, when you turn seventy-three, the government requires you to withdraw a portion of your account, which the IRS calculates based on the size of your account and your estimated lifespan. This required minimum distribution is the government's insurance it will collect some taxes from your earnings at some point. Because you didn't pay taxes on the front end, you will now pay income taxes on whatever you withdraw — including your RMDs.

Let me reiterate something I pointed out in the Longevity chapter. Beginning at age seventy-three, you are required to withdraw a certain minimum amount every year from your 401(k) or IRA, or else you will face a tax penalty on any RMD monies you should have withdrawn but didn't — and that's on top of income tax. The SECURE Act 2.0 reduced the penalty to 25 percent (from 50 percent). Timely corrections also can reduce the penalty to 10 percent.[57]

Even after you begin RMDs, you can still continue contributing to your 401(k) or IRAs if you are still employed, which can affect the whole discussion on RMDs and possible tax considerations. The SECURE Act 2.0 raised the RMD age to seventy-three from seventy-two. In addition, the latest legislation stipulates the

---

[57] Jim Probasco. Investopedia. October 20, 2023. "SECURE 2.0 Act of 2022: Overview, Rules, Limits" https://www.investopedia.com/secure-2-0-definition-5225115

RMD age will increase to seventy-five for those born in 1960 or later.[58]

If you don't need income from your retirement accounts, RMDs can seem like more of a tax burden than an income boon. While some people prefer to reinvest their RMDs, this comes with the possibility of additional taxation: You'll pay income taxes on your RMDs and then potential capital gains taxes on the growth of your investments. If you are legacy-minded, there are other ways to use RMDs, many of which have tax benefits.

### *SECURE 2.0 Act provisions*
In addition to changes imposed for RMD ages, Secure Act 2.0 also expanded access to retirement savings using different methods. Provisions in the legislation go into effect at different times, ranging from 2023-25.

- Beginning January 2, 2024, plan participants can access up to $1,000 (once a year) from retirement savings for emergency, personal, or family expenses without paying a 10-percent early withdrawal penalty.
- Beginning January 2, 2024, employees can establish a Roth emergency savings account of up to $2,500 per participant.
- Beginning January 2, 2024, domestic abuse survivors can withdraw the lesser of $10,000 or 50 percent of their retirement account without penalty.[59]

---

[58] Ibid.
[59] Betterment editors. Betterment. February 24, 2023. "SECURE Act 2.0: Signed into Law" https://www.betterment.com/work/resources/secure-act-2

- Beginning January 1, 2023, victims of a qualified, federally declared disaster can withdraw up to $22,000 from their retirement account without penalty.[60]

## Permanent Life Insurance

One way to turn those pesky RMDs into a legacy is through permanent life insurance. Assuming you need the death benefit coverage and can qualify for it medically, if properly structured, these products can pass on a sizeable death benefit to your beneficiaries — tax-free — as part of your general legacy plan.

The offer of tax-free lifetime benefits has led us to call this approach Specially Designed Life Insurance (SDLI). If structured correctly by a professional, policy owners can defer taxes within the policy and draw them tax-free during the insured's lifetime as a loan in addition to the tax-free death benefit. This little-known method is protected by Section 7702 of the Internal Revenue Code.[61]

## Irrevocable Life Insurance Trust (ILIT)

Another way to use RMDs toward your legacy is to work with an estate planning attorney to create an irrevocable life insurance trust. This is basically a permanent life insurance policy placed within a trust. Because the trust is irrevocable, you would relinquish control of it, but unlike with just a permanent life insurance policy, your death benefit won't count toward your taxable estate.

---

[60] Charlie Pastor. The Motley Fool. February 16, 2023. "Law Opens New Doors for Penalty-Free Retirement Account Distributions" www.fool.com/the-ascent/buying-stocks/articles/law-opens-new-doors-for-penalty-free-retirement-account-distributions
[61] Investopedia. November 29, 2023. "IRS Section 7702: What It Is and Recent Tax Code Changes" https://www.investopedia.com/terms/s/section-7702.asp

### Annuities

Because annuities can be tax-deferred, using all or a portion of your RMDs (after they are taxed) to fund a non-qualified annuity contract can be one way to further delay taxation while guaranteeing your income payments (either to you or your loved ones) later. Of course, this assumes you don't need the RMD income during your retirement. We have seen people who have taxable (or even tax-free) interest or dividends switch those investments to non-qualified annuities to defer all growth and earnings until the time they want to use them, thereby lowering their current income tax or their provisional income used to calculate the taxation level on their Social Security payments (or both). This can be very simple and effective.

### Qualified Charitable Distributions (QCDs)

If you are charity-minded, you may use your RMDs toward a charitable organization instead of using them for income. You must do this directly from your retirement account (you can't take the RMD check and *then* pay the charity) for your withdrawals to be qualified charitable distributions, but this is one way of realizing some of the benefits of a charitable legacy during your own lifetime. You will not need to pay taxes on your QCDs, and they won't count toward your annual charitable tax deduction limit; plus, you'll be able to see how the organization you are supporting uses your donations. You should consult a financial professional on how to correctly make a QCD.

# Roth IRAs

Since the Taxpayer Relief Act of 1997, there has been a different kind of retirement account — or "tax wrapper" — available to the public: the Roth. Roth IRAs and Roth 401(k)s each differ from their traditional counterparts in one big way: You pay your taxes on the front end. Once your post-tax money is in the Roth account, as long as you follow the rules and limitations of that account, your distributions are truly tax-free. You won't pay income tax when you take withdrawals, so in turn, you don't have to worry about RMDs. However, Roth accounts have the same limitations as traditional 401(k)s and IRAs when it comes to withdrawing money before age fifty-nine-and-one-half, with the added stipulation that the account must have been open for at least five years for the account holder to make withdrawals.

# Roth Conversions

Today, there have been many changes to how you can contribute to and use Roth IRAs. Perhaps one of the most important changes allows an investor to convert the pre-tax assets we have been discussing (401(k)s and the like) to a Roth IRA, pay the income taxes due at that time, and then let the Roth IRA grow tax-free for the rest of their lives.[*][62] This can be supremely powerful for paying less income taxes in the long run. As it stands in 2024, there are no income or conversion amount limitations to qualify for Roth conversions. These assets are tax-free for life and also pass income tax-free upon death, making this a generationally effective form of long-term income tax savings for many people. It is important to consult your tax advisor or tax planner to consider the impact of such an approach.

When I have helped people consider this conversion approach, we have been able to project future federal income tax savings in the hundreds of thousands — and in some cases, *millions* — of dollars!

---

[*] Investment growth in the value of a Roth IRA account is not guaranteed or projected, and depends on the success of your investment strategy.
[62] Internal Revenue Service. August 20, 2024. "Roth IRAs" https://www.irs.gov/retirement-plans/roth-iras#

# Taking Charge

As mentioned earlier, the 401(k) and IRA have largely replaced pensions, but they aren't an equal trade.

Pensions are employer-funded; the money feeding into them is money that wouldn't ever show up on your pay stub. Because 401(k)s are self-funded, you must actively and consciously save. This distinction has made a difference when it comes to funding retirement. Fidelity Investments published a study detailing the average 401(k) balance for a person aged fifty-five to sixty-four is $207,874, but the median likely tells the full story. The median 401(k) balance for a person aged fifty-five to sixty-four is $71,168. Those figures reflect Fidelity accounts from the third quarter of 2024.[63]

There can be many reasons why people underfund their retirement plans, like being overwhelmed by investment choices or taking withdrawals from IRAs when they leave an employer. Still, the reason at the top of the list seems to be this: People simply aren't participating to begin with.

So, whether you use a 401(k) with an employer or an IRA alternative with a private company separate from your workplace, the most important retirement savings decision you can make is to sock away your money somewhere in the first place.

---

[63] Arielle O'Shea and Elizabeth Ayoola. NerdWallet. February 16, 2024. "The Average 401(k) Balance by Age"
https://www.nerdwallet.com/article/investing/the-average-401k-balance-by-age

# CHAPTER 8

# Annuities

In my practice, I offer my clients a variety of products — from securities to insurance — designed to help them work toward their financial goals. You may be wondering: Why single out a particular product in this book?

Well, while most of my clients have a pretty good understanding of business and finance, I sometimes find those who have the impression magic must be involved. Some people assume there is a magic finance wand we can wave to change years' worth of savings into a strategy for retirement income. But it's not as easy as a goose laying golden eggs or the Fairy Godmother turning a pumpkin into a coach!

Finances aren't magic; it takes lots of hard work and, typically, several financial products and strategies to pull together a complete retirement plan. Of all the financial products I work with, it seems people find none more mysterious than annuities. And, if I may say, even some of those who recognize the word "annuity" have a limited understanding of the product. So, in the interest of demystifying annuities, let me tell you a little about what an annuity is.

In general, insurance is a financial hedge against risk. Car owners buy auto insurance to protect their finances in case they injure someone or someone injures them. Homeowners have house insurance to protect their homes in case of fire, flood, or another disaster. People have life insurance to help protect their finances in case of untimely death. Almost juxtaposed to life insurance, people have annuities in case of a long life; annuities can give you financial confidence by providing consistent and reliable income payments.

The basic premise of an annuity is you, the annuitant, pay an insurance company some amount in exchange for their contractual guarantee they will pay you income for a certain time period. How that company pays you, for how long, and how much they offer are all determined by the annuity contract you enter into with the insurance company. *However, this is only part of the story with today's annuities.* They are now much more of an investment option that can fulfill the Protect Bucket of a carefully designed custom Spend, Protect, Grow plan.

# The Ways You Can Draw Benefits

There are several ways for an annuity contract to provide income: annuitization, income riders, partial surrenders, and settlement options for heirs.

## Annuitization

When someone "annuitizes" a contract, it is the point where they turn on the income stream. Once a contract has been annuitized, there is no going back. With annuities, if the policyholder lives longer than the insurance company planned, the insurance company is still obligated to pay them, even if the payments end up being way more than the contract's actual value.

If, however, the policyholder dies an untimely death, depending on the contract type, the insurance company may keep anything left of the money that funded the annuity. Nothing would be paid out to the contract holder's survivors. You see where that could make some people balk? Now, modern annuities rarely rely on annuitization for the income portion of the contract and instead have so many bells and whistles that the old concept of annuitization seems outdated, but because this is still an option, it's important to at least understand the basic concept.

In the thirty-six years I have been doing this work, I have only ever annuitized an annuity once! It was for an older widow living in a trailer park with no relatives. All she wanted was to turn her $100,000 into a monthly income she could never outlive, so that's what we did. Other than that one time, thousands of cases later, I have never recommended it. This is significant because the risks of annuitization frequently make the top three reasons why annuities are maligned, yet it is rarely — if ever — done.

## Riders

Speaking of bells and whistles, let's talk about riders. Modern annuities have a lot of different options these days, many in the form of riders you can add to your contract for a fee. The fee typically amounts to 0.1 percent to 1 percent of the contract value per year.[64] Each rider has its particulars, and the types of riders available will vary by the type of annuity contract purchased, but I'll just briefly outline some of these little extras:

- Lifetime income rider: Contract guarantees you an enhanced or flexible income for life
- Death benefit rider: Contract pays an enhanced death benefit to your beneficiaries, even if you have annuitized

---

[64] Shawn Plummer. The Annuity Expert. 2024. "Annuity Fees: What You Need To Know" https://www.annuityexpertadvice.com/types-of-annuities/annuity-fees/

- Return of premium rider: Guarantees you (or your beneficiaries) will at least receive back the premium value of the annuity
- Long-term care rider: Provides a certain amount, sometimes as much as twice the normal income benefit amount for a period of time to help pay for long-term care if the contract holder is moved to a nursing home or assisted living situation

This isn't an extensive look, and usually, the riders have fancier names based on the issuing company, like "Lorem Ipsum Insurance Company Income Preferred Bonus Fixed Index Annuity rider," but I just wanted to show you what some of the general options are in layperson's terms.

## Partial Surrender

Most annuities offer a free withdrawal provision that is often referred to as a partial surrender. An annuity contract typically allows for an annual withdrawal of up to 10 percent, typically, of the account/contract value or of the premium originally paid. The option to make this withdrawal, typically without penalty, can be used as a tool to help with your income planning strategies. Keep in mind, the withdrawal is subject to income taxes and an additional 10 percent IRS penalty if you're under age fifty-nine-and-one-half.

This percentage can be accessed during the surrender period and can be a sound strategy, especially for a client who does not require a regular influx of income provided by a rider. After the surrender value period, the holder of the annuity can access the entire annuity accumulation value without any surrender charges.

I find the partial surrender strategy to often be effective for my clients, particularly if they do not need regular income generated through the use of a rider. A partial surrender allows for the annuity holder to just take out funds when a need arises.

Those who say these are "locked up" too long need to consider the following: When was the last time you needed all of your money on the same day? When was the last time you needed more than 10 percent of it? Most importantly, if you *do* need to withdraw even the free 10 percent we have discussed (allowed by most programs we would ever use) every year, how long would you expect that account to last anyway? For most of our clients, this is plenty of liquidity and invalidates contentious and frequently overblown scare tactics that annuities are "locked up" for ten years.

Ultimately, everything comes down to things like a Written Retirement Income Plan based on your specific income needs and, subsequently, a custom Spend, Protect, Grow allocation to help you safely and logically implement the plan and enjoy the standard of living you desire throughout your lifetime.

## Settlement Options

While any value of an annuity left to beneficiaries upon the annuity holder's death is fairly self-explanatory, there is a point worth raising. Heirs have different settlement options they can consider, including opportunities for lump sums, periodic payments, or specific payouts.

Specific payouts are often based on tax considerations involving a beneficiary or multiple beneficiaries. As an advanced tax planning measure, I have clients who have addressed tax implications with their heirs regarding the most advantageous method for arranging a settlement option that eases any tax burden on the beneficiary.

# Types of Annuities

Annuities break down into four basic types: immediate, variable, fixed, and fixed index.

## Immediate

Immediate annuities primarily rely on annuitization to provide income. You give the insurance company a lump sum up front, and your payments begin immediately. Once you begin receiving income payments, the transaction is irreversible, and you no longer have access to your money in a lump sum. When you die, any remaining contract value is typically forfeited to the insurance company.

All other annuity contract types are "deferred" contracts, meaning you fund your policy as a lump sum or over a period of years. You give it the opportunity to grow over time — sometimes years, sometimes decades.

## Variable

A variable annuity is an insurance contract as well as a security product. It's sold by insurance companies, but only through someone who is also registered to sell security products. With a variable annuity contract, the insurance company invests your premiums in sub-accounts that are tied to the stock market.

This makes it a bit different from the other annuity contract types because it is the only contract where your money is subject to losses because of market declines. Your contract value has a greater opportunity to grow, but it also stands to lose. Additionally, your contract's value will be subject to the underlying investment fees and limitations, including management fees. Once it is time for you to receive income from the contract, if you decide you want to, the insurance company will pay you a certain income, locked in at whatever your contract's value was.*

Insurance carriers may charge mortality and expense (M&E) fees or additional administrative fees to maintain the insurance policy contract, which could lower your contract value. Suffice it to say that today, these types of annuities have endured decades of criticism concerning their overall fee structure, even if that structure is fair based on an annuities' specific benefits.

## Fixed

A traditional fixed annuity is pretty straightforward. You purchase a contract with a guaranteed and fixed interest rate, and if you want, the insurance company will make regular income payments to you at whatever payout rate your contract guarantees. Those payments will continue for the rest of your life and, if you choose, for the remainder of your spouse's life.

Fixed annuities don't typically offer significant upside potential, but many people like them for their guarantees and predictability. After all, if your Aunt Shaun lives to be ninety-five, knowing she has a paycheck later in life can be her mental and financial safety net. Unlike variable annuities, which are subject to market risk and might be up one year and down the next, you can easily calculate the value of your fixed annuity, both yearly and over your lifetime.

## Fixed Index

To recap, variable annuities take on more risk to offer more possibilities to grow. Fixed annuities have less potential growth, but they protect your principal. In the last three decades, many insurance companies have retooled their

---

* A variable annuity is sold by prospectus. Carefully read the prospectus before purchasing a variable annuity.

product line to offer fixed indexed annuities, which are sort of midway between variable and fixed annuities on that risk/reward spectrum. Fixed index annuities offer greater growth potential than traditional fixed annuities but, in some cases, less than variable annuities. Like traditional fixed annuities, however, fixed index annuities are completely protected from downside market losses.

Fixed index annuities earn interest that is tied to an external market index, meaning that instead of your contract value growing at a set interest rate like a traditional fixed annuity, it has the potential to grow within a range. Your contract's value is credited interest based on the performance of an external market index like the S&P 500® while never being invested in the market itself. You can't invest in the S&P 500® directly, but based on when your contract credits interest to your account (e.g., one year — point-to-point, two years — point-to-point, etc.), your annuity has the potential to earn interest based on the chosen index's performance. The earnings may be subject to limits set by the company (such as caps, spreads, and participation rates).

For instance, if your contract caps your interest at 8 percent, then in a year that the S&P 500® gains 5 percent, your annuity value increases 5 percent. If the S&P 500® gains 35 percent, your annuity value gets an 8 percent return. But since your money isn't actually invested in the market with a fixed index annuity, if the market nosedives (such as happened during 2000, 2008, 2020, and 2022, anyone?), you won't see any increase or decrease in your contract value.

That's right — there will also be no decrease in your contract value, no matter how badly the market performs. As long as you follow the terms of the contract, you won't lose any of the interest you were credited in previous years either.

So, what if the S&P 500® shows a market loss of 30 percent? Your contract value isn't going anywhere unless you purchased an optional rider, which has a yearly fee. This rider charge will still come out of your annuity value each year. We have learned that many of our clients do not need or want some of the riders, which must be paid for even in down years, so we rarely use them. For those who are interested in protection and growth potential, fixed index annuities without annual rider costs can be an attractive option. When the stock market has a long period of positive performance, a fixed index annuity can enjoy conservative growth. And during stretches where the stock market is erratic and stock values across the board take significant losses? Fixed index annuities won't lose anything due to the stock market volatility.

It turns out that most people have no idea how truly valuable *not losing principal* is in a long-term investment program. This, combined with better-than-average index offers due to interest rates going way up in the last couple of years, has made fixed index annuities very attractive in 2024 — especially on a relative basis. It also explains why, in 2023, FIA sales went up 23 percent to nearly *$96 billion* in just this one segment of the annuity market.[65]

# Other Things to Know About Annuities

We just explained the four kinds of annuity contracts available, but all of them have some commonalities as annuities.

For all annuities, the contractual guarantees are only as strong as the insurance company that sells the product, which makes

---

[65] Frank Gorshin. Annuity.com. March 28, 2024. "How the Annuity Market Captured $383 Billion in 2023" https://annuity.com/annuities/how-the-annuity-market-captured-385-billion-in-2023/

it important to thoroughly check the credit ratings of any company whose products you are considering. A licensed and qualified financial advisor can help with this.

Annuities invested with after-tax dollars are tax-deferred, meaning you don't have to pay taxes on interest earnings each year as the contract value grows. Instead, you will pay ordinary income taxes first on your withdrawals that are attributable to the earnings only. These are meant to be long-term products, so like other tax-deferred or tax-advantaged products, if you begin taking withdrawals from your contract before age fifty-nine-and-one-half, you may also have to pay a 10 percent federal tax penalty. Also, while annuities are generally considered illiquid, some contracts allow you to withdraw up to 10 percent of your contract value every year, as I mentioned previously. Withdraw any more, however, and you could incur surrender charges.

Keep in mind, your withdrawals will deplete the accumulated cash value, death benefit, and possibly the rider values of your contract.

Annuities aren't for everyone, but it's important to understand them before saying "yea" or "nay" on whether they fit into your plan; otherwise, you're not operating with complete information, wouldn't you agree? Regardless, you should talk to a financial professional who can help you understand annuities, dissect your particular financial needs, and show you whether an annuity is appropriate for your retirement income plan. Also, make sure you stick to the facts versus random internet article scare tactics or money management company ads designed to smear annuities since they do not provide them to clients.

# CHAPTER 9

# Estate and Legacy Planning Strategies

I n my practice, I devote a significant portion of my time to matters of estate and legacy planning strategies. That doesn't mean drawing up wills or trusts or putting together powers of attorney or anything like that. After all, I'm not an estate planning attorney. But I am a financial professional and a Certified Financial Planner®, and what part of the "estate" isn't affected by money matters?

I've included this chapter because I have seen many people do estate planning wrong. Clients, or clients' families, have come in after experiencing a death in the family and have found themselves in the middle of probate, high taxes, or a discovery of something unforeseen (often long-term care) draining the estate.

I have also seen people do estate planning right: clients or families who meet with me proactively to discuss legacies and ways to make them last, and adult children who have room to grieve without an added burden of unintended costs or stress from a family fractured because of inadequate planning.

I'll share some of these stories here. However, I'm not going to give you specific advice, since everyone's situation is unique. I would advise you to speak with an estate planning attorney for specific advice. I only want to give you some things to think about and to underscore the importance of planning ahead.

## You Can't Take It With You

When it comes to legacy and estate planning strategies, the most important thing is to *do it*. I have heard people from clients to celebrities (rap artist Snoop Dogg comes to mind) say they aren't interested in what happens to their assets when they die because they'll be dead. That's certainly one way to look at it. But I think that's a very selfish way to go about things. We all have people and causes we care about, and those who care about us. Even if the people we love don't *need* what we leave behind, they can still be legally tied up in the probate process or burial costs if we don't plan for asset disposition. And that's not even considering what happens if you become incapacitated at some point while you are still alive. Having a plan in place can greatly help reduce the stress of those responsibilities on your loved ones; it's just a loving thing to do.

# Documents

There are a few documents that lay the groundwork for legacy planning. You've probably heard of all or most of them, but I'd like to review what they are and how people commonly use them. These are all things you should talk about with an estate planning attorney to establish your legacy.

## Powers of Attorney (POA)

A power of attorney is a document giving someone the authority to act on your behalf and in your best interests. These come in handy in situations where you cannot be present (think of a vacation where you get stuck overseas) or for durable powers of attorney (DPOA), even when you are incapacitated (think in a coma or coping with dementia).

It is important to have powers of attorney in place and to appoint someone you trust to act on your behalf in these matters. Have you ever heard of someone who was incapacitated after a car accident, whether from head trauma or being in a coma for weeks — sometimes months? Do you think their bills stopped coming due during that time? I like my phone company and my bank, but neither one is about to put a moratorium on sending me bills — particularly not for an extended or interminable period. A power of attorney would have the authority to pay your mortgage or cancel your cable while you are unable to do so.

### *You can have multiple attorneys-in-fact and require them to act jointly.*

What this looks like: Do you think two heads are better than one? One man, Douglas, significantly relied on his two sons' opinions for both his business and personal matters. He appointed both sons as attorneys-in-fact (AIFs), requiring both their signoffs for his medical and financial matters. Ironically, one of them happened to be an attorney by profession, and the other was a doctor!

### *You can have multiple attorneys-in-fact who can act independently.*

What this looks like: Betty had three children with whom she routinely stayed. They lived in different areas of the country, which she thought was an advantage; one month she might be visiting the West Coast, the next she could enjoy a summer month in Cape Cod, and the next she could visit the national monuments in Washington, DC. She named her three children as independently authorized attorneys-in-fact, so if something happened, no matter where she was, the child closest could step in to act on her behalf.

***You can have attorneys-in-fact who have different responsibilities.***
What this looks like: Although Weston's friend Caty, a nurse, was his go-to and attorney-in-fact for health-related issues, financial matters usually made her nervous, so he appointed his good neighbor, Ben, as his attorney-in-fact in all of his financial and legal matters.

In addition to POAs, it may be helpful to have an advanced health care directive (HCD), which is sometimes referenced as a ***living will.*** This is a document where you have pre-decided what choices you would make about different health scenarios. An advanced health care directive can help ease the burden for your medical attorney-in-fact and loved ones, particularly when it comes to end-of-life care.

## Wills

Perhaps the most basic document of legacy planning, a will is a legal document wherein you outline your wishes for your estate. When it comes to your estate after your death, having a will is the foundation of your legacy. Without one, your loved ones are left behind to guess what you would have wanted, and the court will likely split your assets according to the state's probate laws. As far as anyone knows, maybe that's exactly what you wanted, right? Because even if you told your nephew Spencer he could have your car he's been driving, if it's not in writing, it still might go to your brother, sister, son, or daughter to whom you aren't speaking.

However, it may not be enough just to have a will. Even with a will, your assets will be subject to probate. Probate is what we call the state's process for determining a will's validity. A judge will go through your will to question if it conflicts with state law, if it is the most up-to-date document, if you were mentally competent at the time it was in order, etc. For some, this is a quick, easily resolved process. For others, particularly if someone steps forward to contest the will, it may take years to settle, all the while subjecting the assets to court costs and attorney's fees.

One other undesirable piece of the probate process is that it is a public process. That means anyone can go to the courthouse, ask for copies of the case, and discover your assets. They can also see who is slated to receive what and who is disputing.

It's also important to remember beneficiary designations trump wills. So, that large life insurance policy? What if, when you bought it fifteen years ago, you wrote your ex-husband's name on the beneficiary line? Even if you stipulate otherwise in your will, the company that holds your policy will pay out to your ex-spouse. Or how about the thousands of dollars in your IRA you dedicated to the children thirty years ago, but one of your children was killed in a car accident, leaving his wife and two toddlers behind? That IRA is going to transfer to your remaining children, with nothing for your daughter-in-law and grandchildren.

That may paint a grim portrait, but I can't underscore enough the importance of working with a skilled estate planning attorney to keep your will and beneficiary designations up to date as your life changes.

## Trusts

Another piece of legacy planning to consider are trusts. A trust is set up through an attorney who appoints and authorizes a trusted party or trustee(s) to administer the trust (e.g., make decisions, manage the assets in the trust, distribute funds from the trust, etc.) according to the provisions of the trust agreement.

Many people are skeptical of trusts because they assume trusts are only appropriate for the fabulously wealthy. A simple trust will likely cost more than $1,000 if prepared by an estate planning attorney, and fees can be higher for couples.[66] But a trust can help you avoid both the expense and publicity of probate, provide a more immediate transfer of wealth, avoid some taxes, and provide you greater control over your legacy.

For instance, if you want to set aside some funds for a grandchild's college education, you can make it a requirement that they enroll in classes before your trust will dispense any funds. Like a will, beneficiary designations will override your trust conditions, so you still should be keeping your beneficiary designations on insurance policies, investment accounts (e.g., 401(k)s, IRAs, etc.), and other assets up to date.

Like any financial or legal consideration, there are many options these days beyond the simple "yes or no" question of whether to have a trust. For one thing, you will need to consider if you want your trust to be revocable (you can change the terms while you are alive) or irrevocable (can't be changed; you are no longer the "owner" of the contents).

A brief note here about irrevocable trusts: Although they have significant and greater tax benefits, they are still subject to a Medicaid look-back period. If you transfer your assets into an irrevocable trust in an attempt to shelter them from a Medicaid spend-down, you will be ineligible for Medicaid coverage of long-term care for five years. However, an irrevocable trust can avoid both probate and estate taxes, and it can even help protect assets from legal judgments against you.

Another thing to remember when it comes to trusts, in general, is that even if you have set up a trust, you must remember to fund it. In my thirty-six or so years of work, I've had numerous

---

[66] Rickie Houston. SmartAsset. April 5, 2023. "How Much Does It Cost to Set Up a Trust? https://smartasset.com/estate-planning/how-much-does-it-cost-to-set-up-a-trust

clients come to me assuming they have helped protect their assets with a trust. When we talk about taxes and other pieces of their legacy, it turns out they never retitled any assets or changed any paperwork on the assets they wanted in the trust. So, please remember, a trust is just a bunch of fancy legal papers if you haven't followed through on retitling your assets.

# Taxes

Although charitable contributions, trusts, and other tax-efficient strategies can reduce your tax bill, it's unlikely your estate will be passed on entirely tax-free. Yet, when it comes to building a legacy that can last for generations, taxes can be one of the heaviest drains on the impact of your hard work.

For 2024, the federal estate exemption was $13.61 million per individual and $27.22 million for a married couple, with estates facing up to a 40 percent tax rate after that.[67] Currently, the new estate limits are set to increase with inflation until January 1, 2026, when they will "sunset" back to the inflation-adjusted 2017 limits.[68] And that's not taking into account the various state regulations and taxes regarding estate and inheritance transfers.

Another tax concern "frequent flyer": retirement accounts.

Your IRA or 401(k) can be a source of tax issues when you pass away. For one thing, taking funds from a sizeable account can trigger a large tax bill. However, if you leave the assets in the account, there still required minimum distributions (RMDs), which will take effect even after you die. If you pass

---

[67] Katelyn Washington. Kiplinger. November 15, 2023. "What's the 2024 Estate Tax Exemption?" https://www.kiplinger.com/taxes/estate-tax-exemption-amount-increases
[68] Internal Revenue Service. November 22, 2023. "What's New - Estate and Gift Tax" https://www.irs.gov/businesses/small-businesses-self-employed/whats-new-estate-and-gift-tax

the account to your spouse, they can keep taking your RMDs as is, or your spouse can retitle the account in their name and receive RMDs based on their life expectancy. Remember, if you don't take your RMDs, the IRS will take up to 25 percent of your required distribution (10 percent if corrections are made in a timely fashion). You will still have to pay income taxes whenever you withdraw that money. Provisions in the original SECURE Act require anyone who inherits your IRA, with few exceptions (your spouse, a beneficiary less than ten years younger, or a disabled adult child, to name a few), to empty the account within ten years of your death.

Also — and this is a pretty big also — check with an estate planning attorney if you are considering putting your IRA or 401(k) in a trust. An improperly titled beneficiary form for the IRA could mean the difference of thousands of dollars in taxes. This is just one more reason to work with a financial professional, one who can strategically partner with an estate planning attorney and also a tax advisor to diligently check your decisions.

# CHAPTER 10

# Women Retire Too

I help men, women, and families from all walks of life on their journey to and through retirement. However, we want to address the female demographic specifically. Why? To be perfectly blunt, women are more likely to deal with poverty than men when they reach retirement. I wanted to include this chapter to illuminate some relatively overlooked issues women may face in retirement.

The overall poverty rate for women slightly exceeds the rate for men, but among those seventy-five years and older, 13.51 percent of women live at the poverty rate compared to 8.82 percent of men.[69]

The topics, products, and strategies I cover elsewhere in this book are meant to help address retirement concerns for men *and* women, but the dire statistic above is a reminder that much of traditional planning is geared toward men. Male careers, male lifespans, male health care. The bottom line is women's career paths often look much different than men's, so why would their retirement planning look the same?

---

[69] Statista. September 22, 2022. "Poverty rate in the United States in 2021, by age and gender" https://www.statista.com/statistics/233154/us-poverty-rate-by-gender/

Women often embrace different roles and values than men as workers, wives, mothers, and daughters. They are more apt to take on roles as caretakers, thus women are likely to spend portions of their lives making hard shifts between family and careers. Time out of the workforce means less income accumulation for investments and retirement. Also, non-working years count as zeroes when calculating Social Security benefits. Women who strongly value family and community tend to focus on lifetime gifting and legacy funding, sometimes to the detriment of their own lifestyles.

These unique choices, challenges, and hurdles make a solid case that women deserve special consideration from financial professionals. The argument is further promoted by the fact that 69 percent of men in the U.S. age sixty-five and older happen to be married, compared to 47 percent of women in that age classification.[70] Single women don't have the opportunity to capitalize on the resource pooling and potential economies of scale accompanying a marriage or partnership.

# Be Informed

With all the couples I've seen, there is almost always an "alpha" when it comes to finances. It isn't always men. For many of my coupled clients, the wife is the alpha (the CFO of the family) who keeps the books and budgets and knows where all of the family's assets are, down to the penny. Yet, statistically, among baby boomers, it is usually a man who runs the books. But as time goes on, it looks like the ratio of male to female financial alphas is evening out, based on my experience speaking with couples.

---

[70] Administration for Community Living. November 30, 2022. "Profile of Older Americans" https://acl.gov/aging-and-disability-in-america/data-and-research/profile-older-americans

Because most of the baby boomer alphas are men, there is an all too familiar scene in many financial offices across the country: A woman comes into an appointment carrying a sack full of unopened envelopes. Often through tears, she sits across the desk from a financial professional and apologizes her way through a conversation about what financial products she owns and where her income is coming from. She is recently widowed and was sure her spouse was taking care of the finances, but now she doesn't know where all their assets are kept, and her confidence in her financial outlook has wavered after walking through funeral expenses and realizing she's down to one income.

Often, she may be financially "okay." Yet, the uncertainty can be wearying, particularly when the family is already reeling from a loss. While this scenario sometimes plays out with men, in my experience, it's more likely to be a woman in that chair across from my desk. Although the practice has been leveling more and more in recent decades, for centuries Western traditions held money management down as being "a guy thing." But it doesn't have to be this way. This all-too-common scenario can be wiped away with just a little preparation.

## Talk to Your Spouse/Work with a Financial Professional

While there are many factors affecting women's financial preparation for and situation in retirement, I cannot emphasize enough that the decision to be informed, to be a part of the conversation, and to be aware of what is going on with your finances is absolutely paramount to a confident retirement.

The breakdown regarding couples and finances seems to happen because of a lack of communication. The financial alpha is often the only one who knows how much the family has and where it is invested. Sometimes, it's just a relationship's defacto division of labor, though it may never have been overtly agreed to. In the end, it doesn't matter who handles the money; it's about *all* parties being informed of what's going on financially. In my practice, as soon as I notice one person seems to be the financial alpha, I will deliberately address the other person periodically to get their perspective on things and ensure their point of view is adequately represented. It does not take long for the alpha to notice this, and that effort is generally respected and appreciated.

There are a lot of ways to open the conversation about money. One woman, Lorna, started a conversation with her husband, the financial alpha, by sitting down and saying, "Teach me how to be a widow." Perhaps that sounds grim, but it was to the point, and it spurred what she said was a very fruitful conversation. Couples sometimes have their first real conversation about money, assets, and their retirement income approach in my presence. The important thing about having these conversations isn't where — it's when. The best "when" is as soon as possible.

Lorna told me that after they got the conversation rolling, she and her husband spent a day — just one part of an otherwise dull weekend — going through everything she might need to know. They spent the better part of two decades together after that. When he died and she was widowed, she said the "widowhood" talk had made a huge difference. She knew whom to call to talk through their retirement plan and where to call for the insurance policy.

She said the benefit of the weekend exercise they engaged in some twenty years earlier couldn't have been more apparent than when she ultimately accompanied a recently widowed friend to a financial appointment. Her friend was emotional the whole time, afraid she would run out of money any day. The financial professional ultimately showed the friend that she was financially in good shape, but not before the friend had already spent months worried that each check would exhaust her bank account. That's no way to live after losing a loved one. It was preventable had her deceased spouse and financial professional included her in a conversation about "widowhood."

## Spouse-Specific Options

One area where it might be especially important to be on the same page between spouses is when it comes to financial products or services that have spousal options. A few that come to mind are pensions and Social Security, although life insurance and annuity policies also have the potential to affect both spouses.

With pensions, taking the worker's life-only option is somewhat attractive. After all, the monthly payment is bigger. However, you and your spouse should discuss your options. When we're talking about both of you as opposed to just one lifespan, there is an increased likelihood at least one of you will live a long, long time. This means the monthly payout will be less, but it also helps ensure that no matter which spouse outlives the other, no one will have to suffer the loss of a needed pension paycheck in their later retirement years.

While we covered Social Security options in a different chapter, I think some of the spousal information bears repeating. Particularly, if you worked exclusively inside the home for a significant number of years, you may want to talk about taking your Social Security benefits based on your spouse's work history. After all, Social Security is based on your thirty-five highest-earning years.

Things to remember about the spousal benefits:[71]

---

[71] Social Security Administration. 2024. "Benefits For Your Family" https://www.ssa.gov/benefits/retirement/planner/applying7.html

- Your benefit will be calculated as a percentage (up to 50 percent) of your spouse's earned monthly benefit at their full retirement age (or FRA).
- For you to begin receiving a spousal benefit, your spouse must have already filed for their benefits, and you must be at least sixty-two.
- You can qualify for a full half of your spouse's benefits if you wait until you reach FRA to file.
- Beginning your benefits earlier than your FRA will reduce your monthly check, but waiting to file until after FRA will not increase your benefits.

For divorcees:[72]

- You may qualify for an ex-spousal benefit if ...
    a. You were married for a decade or more
    b. *and* you are at least sixty-two
    c. *and* you have been divorced for at least two years
    d. *and* you are currently unmarried
    e. *and* your ex-spouse is sixty-two (qualifies to begin taking Social Security)
- Your ex-spouse does not need to have filed for you to file on their benefit.
- Similar to spousal benefits, you can qualify for up to half of your ex-spouse's benefits if you wait to file until your FRA.
- If your ex-spouse dies, you may file to receive a widow/widower benefit on their Social Security record, as long as you are at least age sixty and fulfill all the other requirements on the preceding alphabetized list.
    a. This will not affect the benefits of your ex-spouse's current spouse

---

[72] Ibid.

For widow's (or widower's, for that matter) benefits:[73]

- You may qualify to receive as much as your deceased spouse would have received if …
    a. You were married for at least nine months before their death
    b. *or* you would qualify for a divorced spousal benefit (if you were divorced and your ex-spouse dies)
    c. *and* you are at least sixty
    d. *and* you did not/have not remarried before age sixty
- You may earn delayed credits on your spouse's benefit *if* your spouse hadn't already filed for benefits when they died.
- Other rules may apply to you if you are disabled or are caring for a deceased spouse's dependent or disabled child.

# Longevity

On average, women live longer than men. Most stats put average female longevity at about two years more than men. But averages are tricky things. An April 2022 report by the World Economic Forum listed the eight oldest people in the world as being all women. They ranged in age from 114 years old to 118 and included two Americans.[74]

On one hand, women all have unique personalities, goals, ambitions, and passions. However, they share biological and

---

73 Social Security Administration. 2024. "If You Are the Survivor" https://www.ssa.gov/benefits/survivors/ifyou.html
74 Martin Armstrong. World Economic Forum. April 29, 2022. "How old are the world's oldest people?" https://www.weforum.org/agenda/2022/04/the-oldest-people-in-the-world/

instinctual traits that, in general, give rise to longer lives. And, on that note, the trend for women to live longer presents longstanding financial ramifications.

## Simply Needing More Money in Retirement

Living longer in retirement means needing more money. Period. Barring a huge lottery win or some crazy stock market run-up, the date you retire may likely be the point at which you have the most money you will ever have. Not to put too grim a spin on it, but the problem with longevity is the further you get away from that date, the further your dollars have to stretch. If you only planned to live to a nice eighty-something but instead live to a nice 100-something, that is *two decades* you will need to account for monetarily. The "planner" in my CFP® title says to always be conservative with your assumptions so your client will not be disappointed.

To put this in perspective, let's say you like to drink coffee as an everyday splurge. Not accounting for inflation or leap years, a $4 cup-a-day habit is $29,200 over a two-decade span. Now, think of all the things you like to do that cost money. Add those up for twenty years of unanticipated costs. I think you'll see what I mean.

## More Health Care Needs

In addition to the cost of living for a longer lifespan is the fact that aging — plain and simple — means more health care, and more health care means more money. Women are survivors. They suffer from the morbidity-mortality paradox, which states women suffer more non-fatal illnesses throughout their lifetime than men, who experience fewer illnesses but higher mortality sooner.

Women have been found to seek treatment more often when not feeling well and emphasize staying healthy when older, according to studies. Survival, I believe, is on the side of the woman. However, surviving things (such as cancer) also means more checkups later in life.

A statistical concern for women involves the prospect of long-term care. Long-term care for women lasts 3.7 years on average compared to 2.2 years for men.[75]

## Widowhood

Not only do women typically live longer than their same-age male counterparts, but they also stand a greater chance of living alone as they age. Some divorce, separate, or never marry. Among those age sixty-five and over, 33 percent of women live alone compared to 20 percent of men.[76]

I don't write this to scare people; rather, I think it's fundamentally important to prepare my female clients for something that may be a startling *but very possible* scenario. At some point, most women will have to handle their financial situations on their own. For those who may not be so inclined, a little preparation can go a long way, and having a basic understanding of your household finances and the "who, what, where, and how much" of your family's assets is incredibly useful. It can prevent a tragic situation from being more traumatic.

In my opinion, the financial services industry sometimes underserves women in these situations. Some financial professionals tend to alienate women, even when their spouses

---

[75] Lindsay Modglin. SingleCare. January 24, 2024. "Long-term care statistics 2024" https://www.singlecare.com/blog/news/long-term-care-statistics/

[76] Statista. November 23, 2022. "Share of senior households living alone in the United States 2020, by gender" https://www.statista.com/statistics/912400/senior-households-living-alone-usa/

are alive. I've heard several stories of women who sat through meeting after meeting without their financial professional ever addressing a single question to them — so hard to fathom in this day and age.

In our firm, when we work with couples, we work hard to make sure our retirement income strategies work for *both* people. No matter who the financial alpha is, it's important for everyone affected by a retirement strategy to understand it. When training new advisors, I always taught them to address the least engaged person. If that person asks and answers questions and can summarize what is being recommended and why, then the advisor will know the job has been done right.

### *Taxes*

One of the often-unexpected aspects of widowhood is the tax bill. Many women continue similar lifestyles to the ones they shared with their spouses. This, in turn, means continuing to have a similar need for income. However, after the death of a spouse, their taxes will be calculated based on a single filer's income table, which is much less forgiving than the couple's tax rates. This can be a very sobering discovery if not anticipated. With proper planning, your financial professional and tax advisor may be able to help you take the sting out of your new tax status.

# Caregiving

In addition to the financial burden created by caregiving responsibilities, many women often devote hours each day to duties around the home and looking after loved ones. So then, when can women find the time to focus long and hard on financial matters?

Unfortunately, the impact and hardships created by traditional roles for women typically do not account for Social Security benefit losses or the losses of health care benefits and retirement savings. This also doesn't account for maternity care, mothers who homeschool, or women who leave the workforce to care for their children in any way.

I don't repeat these statistics to scare you. In America, about 53 million serve as unpaid caregivers and spend roughly $7,000 annually on out-of-pocket caregiving costs.[77] Yet, I think the emotional value of the care many women provide their elderly relatives or neighbors cannot be quantified. So, to be clear, this shouldn't be taken as a "why not to provide caregiving" spiel. Instead, it should be seen as a call for "why to *prepare* for caregiving" or "how to lessen the financial and emotional burden of caregiving."

## Funding Your Own Retirement

For these reasons, women should be prepared to fund more of their own retirements. There are several savings options and products, including the spousal IRA. They are like a typical IRA except used by a person who's married. The working spouse must earn at least as much money as is contributed into the IRA.[78] This is something to consider, particularly for families where one spouse has dropped out of the workforce to care for a relative. Also, if you find yourself in a caregiving role, talk to your employer's human resources department. Some companies have paid leave, special circumstances, or sick leave options you could qualify for, making it easier to cope and helping you stay longer in the workforce.

---

[77] The Scan Foundation. November 10, 2022. "Family caregivers are unsung heroes" https://www.thescanfoundation.org/the-buzz/family-caregivers-are-unsung-heroes

[78] Andrea Coombes. NerdWallet. November 2, 2023. "Spousal IRA: What It Is, How to Open One" https://www.nerdwallet.com/article/investing/spousal-ira-what-it-is-and-why-you-should-open-one

## Saving Money

Women likely need more money to fund their retirements. But this doesn't have to be a significant burden. Often, women are better at saving while usually taking less risk in their portfolios. One source identified many ways in which women are crushing this retirement component.[79]

- In a 2021 analysis of five million Fidelity customers over a ten-year period, women's investment rates of return outperformed men by .04 percent.
- Wells Fargo found that women take approximately 82 percent of the risk men take.
- Meghan Railey, co-founder and CEO of Optas Capital, wrote, "While we have found that male clients tend to eagerly invest in the latest asset class everyone is talking about, like cryptocurrency, female clients do not generally jump on the shiny bandwagon."
- Women do a better job buying and holding quality stocks and avoid impulsive decisions. Staying invested for the long haul is often cited as the most effective investing strategy.
- Women remain calm and are less likely to liquidate their retirement accounts during market volatility.
- Lastly, Vanguard found women are less active investors, logging on to their accounts half as often as men and trading 40 percent less frequently.

With all the hurdles to retirement that are unique to women, it's exciting they inherently have an advantage when it comes to saving. This gives me reason to believe as women get more involved in their finances, families will continue to become more confident about retirement.

---

[79] Lyle Daly. The Motley Fool. February 20, 2024. "Investing for Women: What You Should Know"
https://www.fool.com/research/women-in-investing-research/

# CHAPTER 11

# Finding a Financial Professional

Managing risk to your money and other assets and understanding and mitigating market volatility in retirement is vital. You should not do it alone — that is a real risk and why so many Americans materialize their worst fear: Running out of money during their lifetime.

You need a financial professional willing to call in other appropriate experts (like tax specialists or estate planning attorneys) to help you reach your goals — and to keep as much of your money as possible.

In my observation, people make five main mistakes when retirement is at hand. And again, a certified financial planning professional can help you avoid them.

## Five Mistakes Putting Your Retirement at Risk

The first fundamental mistake people make regarding retirement is *not consulting a professional* or waiting too long to do so. You need to sit down with a professional. The risks of making expensive mistakes by being a do-it-yourselfer are far too high.

These DIYers believe they can do anything better themselves. I've seen that the more educated an investor is, the more likely they are to be a do-it-yourselfer — and make costly mistakes with their money. They might consult experts but tend to know — almost in advance — that they'll never take their advice or use their services. I cannot stress this enough: *Please* admit that there are things you've probably never heard of and others where your knowledge may be dated. Things move and change in the worlds of finance, investing, taxation, and even legacy planning. And did I mention inflation? You need to consult (and, I might add, listen to and act on the advice of) a financial planning professional.

The second common mistake people make is mistrusting, then rejecting, the power of *annuities*. This happens when what people believe or "know" about today's most effective products and strategies is either outdated, misrepresented, or just plain false. Let me emphasize: Don't believe everything you read online, even if it appears to be from a credible source. McAdam's independent advisors have truly vetted all of today's products; our team continuously studies old and new products to identify the best of the best. We will only present the outstanding ones to create a powerful strategy for your goals and needs.

The third mistake arises from emotions — particularly fear, We call it *financial decision-making paralysis*. When we sit with clients for an annual or periodic review, we note if there have been significant changes in any part of their five plans. If so, we'll recommend reorganizing their finances to protect their assets — and they'll hesitate! We recognize when a client is about to make this mistake when they say things like, "Well, you know, Phil, this is the way we've always done it, and it's worked for us so far," or, "I just don't want to make a mistake, and if I don't change anything, then I probably won't make a mistake." Everything about finances and money can change — tax rates, laws governing how you manage your estate, stock market volatility, inflation, etc. *Listen to your informed advisor.*

The fourth mistake most of the investing public makes is *not optimizing their lifetime tax picture.* Frankly, I don't know anyone who can achieve this alone. This is a real risk to your retirement.

Say a new client sits with me, saying, "Phil, I have $2.75 million for retirement. It's still in my 401(k) account." Well, no. This person does *not* have $2.75 million for retirement. They have not yet looked at their tax plan with a specialist, much less the other four plans they'll need to de-risk their retirement properly. People in our country tend to gravitate like moths to the proverbial flame toward lowering their income taxes in the *current* year versus thinking about the future *lifetime* income tax situation they might encounter. It's a mistake that can deplete your assets of hundreds of thousands — sometimes *millions* — of dollars. Don't make that mistake. Consult us. Play the long game and learn how to pay less taxes over your lifetime. And, as we always recommend, please consult your tax advisor.

The fifth mistake we see people making is (like the others I've listed) the very opposite of de-risking their retirement. It's the belief that "high risk means high returns" because when you invest in a high-flying, fast-growing stock, it reaches the moon. Was taking that huge risk what made you the huge profits? Hopefully.

Investors beware: Only investors who have *many years* until retirement should expose themselves to more volatility and risk in this manner. The strategy is that, with many years before retirement, volatility is your friend and can lead to a bigger pot of gold when you retire. But close to or during retirement?

Don't make this mistake. If your risky bet should fail, your wealth could evaporate. Just one or two bad years early in retirement can ruin what could have been a long, successful retirement for most folks. As I mentioned earlier, the phenomenon that explains the impact of the order and depth of a market downturn at an inopportune time (such as in early retirement) is referred to as "sequence of returns" risk. It is the primary reason why the "4 Percent Rule" of retirement withdrawal is no longer relevant. This sequence of returns risk has a solution: the Spend, Protect, Grow paradigm helps maintain a high standard of living for a lifetime!

A good advisor will be familiar with the above mistakes. Put all the good cards in your hand — consult with professionals before making any financial decisions.

## Holistic Planning

To further de-risk your financial retirement, we prepare our five interdependent plans: income, health care, investments, taxes, and legacy.

First, we establish your retirement *income* goals, including expenses such as *health care* as you age. Then, we examine your *investments*, their location, and the *tax* effects (how to reduce taxes strategically over your lifetime). We discuss your thoughts and wishes for a *legacy*, then look at how to achieve that so heirs and beneficiaries receive more and pay less tax as well.

Will you need all the plans at once? Perhaps not. Perhaps you haven't made legacy decisions yet or need more information before putting your health care provisions on paper. Eventually, though, you *will* need the five plans. That is maximum de-risking at its finest.

But what's more, it won't be a one-and-done planning process. Come in every year. Let us review it all. Your health status may have changed. Newly enacted probate laws require a review of your plans, and it's the same with tax laws. Perhaps inflation has surged, and we need to revise your Spend, Protect, Grow plan. These reviews ensure that you are and remain de-risked to the degree possible.

As we work with you, we combine and integrate McAdam's three uniques — *Holistic Advisor, Safe Money Strategies*, and *Process-Driven Portfolio Management* — into all five plans we prepare with you.

We also deploy our analytical tools to magnify how you should (re)organize your money's allocation or location (perhaps both!) for maximum de-risking and longevity of your assets.

You need all five plans. You need regular, frequent reviews with your advisor. It's a volatile world full of unknowns— the only constant is change. Since Mike McAdam founded our firm, we have been de-risking clients' financial positions as much as possible by planning for all the contingencies that can occur during their lives.

## Combining the Three Uniques

I've told you about McAdam's three uniques. Only 1 percent of planners in our industry offer the *combination* of all three. Because we use them in an integrated manner, McAdam advisors have a more effective holistic approach to helping you:

1. Find a *Holistic Advisor* who does fee-based financial planning and then implements that work independently to choose from the best products and services offered across the nation
2. Work with an advisor with expertise in *Safe Money Strategies*

3. Engage a *proprietary, process-driven portfolio/wealth management* approach that's unique in the marketplace

It is very difficult to locate other firms that do all these things. Come to McAdam for a "one-stop-shop" experience for all your financial needs. You will not regret it!

# Frequently Asked Questions

These are questions you should frequently ask, and our direct answers:

### What is the biggest issue you face helping people achieve a comfortable retirement?

That would be the general lack of awareness of so many investors. There are many things people are unaware of, including:

- Certain products and strategies ideally suited for them
- The qualifications or biases of writers who put information on the internet
- Changes in products that used to be unattractive but are now desirable
- The need to change from paradigms best deployed for long-term saving toward retirement to those best aligned with short- and long-term spending in retirement
- The difference between a practicing Certified Financial Planner® and a money manager or product salesperson

### How do I know if I can trust you?

How have you made the same decision about working with other important advisors (like doctors, accountants, or attorneys)? If possible, you might get a referral from a friend. Otherwise, research the person you are considering. Look at their experience level and whether they have massive complaints lodged against them (either formal or in the form of reviews). Once you have gathered enough relevant information about how well you think they can relate to you and your concerns, make a decision!

Stop saying you need to think about things for months. If you really think about it, that procrastination reflects that you simply don't want to make a decision. Not making a decision (or essentially not making changes) is still a decision itself, and it's often not the best one.

### Why would I change any of my actions if they got me to where I am today?

I think knowing when to change — and actually committing to making changes — is hard for most people. Some need to experience the pain of not changing before becoming motivated to make changes. This can sometimes come way too late! In the financial world, people typically have the most money they've ever had when they retire. This can magnify mistakes to their extreme, and sometimes, it's too late at that point to fix them.

Use logic to process new paradigms that are well-suited to replace the old ones and try to remove emotion. Change does not invalidate how you got where you are or even cast any shade upon your progress — it merely distinguishes those who will continue to succeed by evolving as needed from those who stubbornly find it noble to go down with the ship instead of changing course. Don't allow yourself to become this person!

### Who should I listen to?

Few things in life are more evident to me than the difference between people who value an unqualified friend's opinion over that of a highly qualified and experienced professional.

I prefer medical analogies to all others here to express how critical this is. Suppose you had a rare form of life-threatening cancer. Would you most value treatment recommendations from a friend, a few articles you found on the internet written by someone you don't know anything about, or the opinion of a seasoned doctor with more than three decades of experience in treating the disease?

This is a no-brainer. Stop asking your friends what they think about things they know almost nothing about. Stop reading articles about rules of thumb. Seek out and then follow advice from qualified professionals familiar with your situation.

### *What are your fees?*
Every single article on the internet that references how to choose the right advisor always says to ask about fees — and you should. However, one key tip is when you don't truly understand the differences between any product or service, the lowest common denominator always tends to be price. You don't *always* want the cheapest options, but we tend to gravitate to that approach when we can't differentiate between products and services, right?

As a person near or in retirement, think about the larger, more essential goods you have purchased — things like your most recent house, car, or major appliance. Did you buy the cheapest one you could find? Of course not! Why would you think any differently when choosing someone to help you retire comfortably and *stay* that way? Price matters, but if it's the only factor you're considering, you won't get the best, most comprehensive, and experienced providers — *period*. So, how do you navigate this?

There are two things to remember. The first is whether you are seeking a comprehensive (holistic) planning advisor or just a money or asset manager. For retirement planning, I highly recommend a comprehensive financial planner. Some people charge fees for this service, and some do not.

There are only three reasons a person does not charge a fee for this (if they do it at all):

1. They are not good at it, and they know it, so they don't charge anything for it.
2. They are not licensed to charge a fee for financial planning advice. One *must* have a license.
3. They (or their company) don't care about planning because they are just product salespeople or money managers (same thing) and are not equipped to help you meet long-term goals through a rigorous planning process. If you truly need advice, be prepared to pay something for it.

The second thing to remember is how financial products are priced in today's marketplace. There are only three basic models for this:

1. Pay something up front (a commission) for a financial product or service, but nothing along the way and nothing when you leave.
2. Pay nothing upfront, pay some percentage annually as you go, and pay nothing when you leave. This is the most well-known approach that money managers tend to use.
3. There is a third approach available for some products that is not well understood but worth knowing about for the cost-conscious among us. You pay nothing upfront, nothing along the way each year, and nothing when you leave! Yep, you read that correctly. The only kicker is that you generally need to leave the bulk of the investment in the product (typically for ten years) to achieve this.

Whenever I say this, people always jump to the conclusion that all that money is "locked up" in the third option above. Not necessarily! The products we use for this today mostly have 10 percent annual free withdrawals. Anything above a 10 percent withdrawal would usually be subject to a surrender fee — which would never be a good idea! And, of course, you do not put all your money in these Safe Money Strategies (annuities). If you are retired and can remove a full 10 percent from any (or even all) of your investments, when would you ever need more than that? To put it another way, if you take 10 percent out of something every year, it wouldn't last for a thirty-year (or longer) retirement anyway!

Pay close attention to "price" when evaluating advisors. At McAdam, we are neither the cheapest nor most expensive in the marketplace, but by all accounts, we *will* provide excellent advice and service for a very fair price.

# Acknowledgments

No one gets to where they are alone. I have many to acknowledge and thank.

First, I want to acknowledge my dad and mom. My father, the late Constantine B. Simonides, came over from Athens, Greece, with the American Field Service on a full scholarship to the Saint Andrews School in Delaware. He went on to MIT, Boston University (where he met my mom, the late Betty L. Simonides), and finally, Harvard Business School. To say he was influential in people's lives was an understatement. He was a talented and charismatic leader who was greatly respected for decades at MIT, where he served as vice president for most of his career. He taught me how to write, communicate, and, ultimately, charm the people around me. He also taught me how to be a leader and to always expect the best of myself and others. He was larger than life when he spoke to groups of people. I have always hoped to become 10 percent of the man he was to me.

My mom, Betty, also had a significant influence on me. She was an extremely successful real estate broker in my hometown of Wellesley Hills, Massachusetts, for thirty years. She was persuasive! She would always find creative ways to get people to agree with her. She was also very talented in performance art and could sing, dance, and act. When I was little, people would come over to the house, and I would sing, dance, or perform somehow, which she deeply encouraged. Most of the people in my life today would argue that none of this has changed!

My older brother, Ted, is a kind and caring soul, and my younger sister, Cindy, always laughed at my jokes. But those two could put me in my place at a moment's notice by recounting some of my antics in their own shameless yet playful ways! They, too, always appreciated me for who I am.

My wife, Shaun, and my three adult children, Jordan (twenty-nine), Weston (twenty-seven), and London (twenty-three), have been a constant source of both love and pride in my life. My only grandson (so far), Colgate, has the unique ability to make my day in less than three seconds when he smiles at me. Who among us can ever amount to anything without the enduring love and support of family? I am prouder of my family — who each of them has become — than I am of any of my own career accomplishments.

Professionally, Scott "Digi" DiGiammarino probably taught me the most and in the fastest way. He was my brother's college roommate, and when I joined the company that later became Ameriprise (AMP), he was my Field Trainer and District Manager. He was very financially successful and about the most fun human being on the planet, making him the reason I joined the company. This was how I made decisions at twenty-three! Digi taught me everything about personal interaction in the financial services business. He had great people instincts, and he made things fun. We made quite a duo for twenty-five years before he retired from financial services. I will always have incredible memories of our reign at Ameriprise!

Larry Post was my first Field and (then later) Group Vice President at Ameriprise. No one was a better salesperson than he was. Fearless and determined, he made everyone around him good at sales. He both led and followed through process and scripting, making me a lifetime believer in the power of both. He ultimately trained and promoted a generation of leaders at Ameriprise who have run that company for decades since. He was a "kingmaker" and yet humble and unpretentious. Everything he did paid off, and people everywhere in our industry can recount the time and things they learned from him. He is nothing short of an American success story, coming from very little and humbly building extraordinary wealth for himself and others.

When I joined the original version of Ameriprise in 1988, Doug Lennick was the General Sales Manager. He knew exactly how to connect with and motivate people. It soon became apparent that they needed more of a numbers-driving sales leader in his position, but they kept him in the fold for decades in roles where he essentially built highly effective leaders and followers like no other. An author, among other things, he was a gifted resource in helping folks tackle their most challenging work-life balance issues in pursuit of high goals.

In 2007, I had my worst year as a Field Vice President out of the eight I had spent in the role. I was losing people left and right and desperate to succeed. I reached out to Doug, and we had a couple of phone calls. He referred me to a few books to read and got me to change how I organized my work and life habits. He helped me implement some very difficult things that I was scared to face at the time. Not only did I turn it around that year, but I won the coveted Outstanding Leader of the Year Award in 2008 in the Field Vice President category. It still amazes me how one caring person could help someone struggling to change so much in just a few months. He remains a special resource to people in our industry today.

Mike McAdam, our firm's CEO, founder, and namesake, has had a lasting effect on me. While we were both at AMP, he (as my junior) was quickly building a name for himself and then had the guts to leave in 2008 to start his own financial services firm — right in the middle of the Great Recession! In just three short years, he built our flagship office in Center City, Philadelphia, to over fifty advisors and staff — at which point he came for me. In one of our famous discussions, he said, "Phil, this thing is coming apart at the seams; I cannot train people fast enough. When we were both at Ameriprise, you were always the speaker on leadership development. I need you to come here, build us a leadership development program, start an office for McAdam in DC (where you live), and help me build this company. I kept everything we loved at AMP, got rid of everything we hated, and went and got everything else we wished we had — and I'll pay you to do it." Sold!

In the nearly fourteen years since then, we have been to a lot of places together. We grew the company by adding both Boston and Chicago locations, and we increased our group to close to 250 people at its peak before COVID-19. All of the leaders of the Northern Virginia, Boston, and Chicago offices were trained, developed, and promoted by me — which is still a source of great pride.

When Covid hit, we had to change many things. I gave up running the offices and my seat on the Executive Team to return to client-facing advising again. Mike asked me to run seminars and go on our most demanding and wealthiest client cases while building a team around me to help me do it. As the most senior person in our firm by any measure, he promoted me to Executive Vice President.

One of the things I respect most about Mike is his fearlessness in pursuing his vision. He could see the potential associated with me changing my role long before I could, and he was determined to help me get to a place where my role could impact the firm's growth in a meaningful way. By then, he knew who I was and the best way to release my potential. I will be forever grateful for his patience, influence, and dedication of resources to get me where I am today.

Thank you for allowing me to share my journey so far, along with the financial practices and paradigms I have been fortunate to have honed along the way. And yet, like so many of us, I remain just another work in progress ...

I'd love to hear your questions, comments, or feedback about the book. Please feel free to reach out to me at:

**philsimonides@mcadamfa.com**

# *About the Author*

**Phil Simonides, CFP®**
**McAdam Financial**

P hil Simonides, CFP®, is the Executive Vice President and a Senior Financial Advisor at McAdam. He is based out of the firm's Tyson's Corner office in Northern Virginia, where his personal practice focuses on high-net-worth individuals and businesses. Phil specializes in retirement planning, wealth management, tax diversification, divorce settlement planning, estate planning, and Safe Money Strategies. He is particularly passionate about wealth preservation.

Phil serves as a spokesman for the firm, having appeared in media outlets such as *The Wall Street Journal*, CNBC, *Bloomberg Radio*, *InvestmentNews*, and *Financial Advisor* magazine. He has been a regular contributor to the Kiplinger's Wealth Creation platform.

He joined McAdam in 2011 after spending much of his thirty-six-year career at Ameriprise Financial, where he last served as Complex Director for the Washington, DC, metropolitan area. While at Ameriprise, he was a Senior Financial Advisor in the firm's Advanced Advisor Group and, most notably, won the coveted national Outstanding Leader Award for Field Vice Presidents in 2008.

### Licenses and Certifications
- Certified Financial Planner (CFP®)
- Registered Principal
- Registered Investment Advisor Representative
- Licensed General Securities Representative
- Municipal Fund Securities Principal
- Registered Options Principal
- Life and Health Insurance Licensed in the District of Columbia, Maryland, Virginia, and many other states.
- Holds Series 4, 7, 24, 51, 52, 63, 65, and SIE licenses

### Personal
Phil is a graduate of Middlebury College. He and his wife live in Great Falls, Virginia, and have three adult children and one grandchild. He is an avid tennis player, pickleball player, and golfer. Phil is also devoted to his community, has served on youth sports boards, and has coached many youth sports. For more than fifteen seasons, he was the voice of Langley High School lacrosse and football in McLean, Virginia. Over the last twenty-five years, Phil has invested considerable time in many local and national charitable and not-for-profit organizations, primarily as a charity auctioneer, event emcee, and board

member. To date, he has raised over $2.5 million from live auctioneer activities alone.

# McAdam

**M**cAdam empowers prospective and existing clients to achieve their dream retirement. Partner with a fiduciary financial advisor from one of our Boston, Chicago, Philadelphia, or Northern Virginia office locations to craft a personalized roadmap, culminating in a written retirement plan tailored to your financial goals and risk tolerance.

This includes comprehensive strategies like retirement planning, 401(k) optimization, tax and insurance analysis, investment planning, education planning, estate planning, and employer benefits optimization. We provide specialized strategies designed to grow, sustain, and protect your wealth, helping to give you peace of mind as you navigate toward a secure retirement.

As a nationally recognized firm, McAdam has received numerous awards, including:*
- USA Today's Best Financial Advisory Firms in 2023 and 2024
- Inc. 5000's America's Fastest-Growing Private Companies in 2017, 2020, 2021, 2022, 2023, and 2024
- AdvisoryHQ's Top Rated Wealth Management Firms of 2020-2021

Let's talk about what matters to you. Schedule your complimentary consultation to begin customizing your own Spend, Protect, Grow plan today!

**Phone:** (888)-227-7162
**General Email:** consultation@mcadamfa.com
**Web:** www.mcadamfa.com

---

* See following pages for award disclosures.

Awards, rankings, ratings, and/or recognition by unaffiliated rating services and/or publications are not indicative of McAdam's future performance, and should not be construed by a client or prospective client as a guarantee that such client will experience a certain level of results if McAdam is engaged, or continues to be engaged to provide investment advisory services, nor should they be construed as a current or past endorsement of McAdam by any of its clients.

Rankings published by magazines and others generally base their selections exclusively on information prepared and/or submitted by the recognized adviser. Such awards, rankings, ratings, and/or recognition are no guarantee of future investment success. Working with a highly-rated advisor does not ensure that a client or prospective client will experience a higher level of performance. Generally, rankings are based on information prepared and submitted by the adviser.

The awards listed do not require memberships or payment for consideration. By virtue of disclosing an award ranking, McAdam is disclosing favorable ratings (to the extent that McAdam is ranked above other advisors) and unfavorable ratings (to the extent that McAdam is ranked below other advisors). The awards and rankings are independently granted. McAdam is not affiliated with the awarding rating services and/or publications listed.

*Inc. 5000 Fastest Growing Companies*
Inc. Magazine is a New York-based publication owned by Mansueto Ventures, Inc. Inc. Magazine produces annual rankings of the fastest-growing privately held companies in the United States. The 2024 Inc. 5000 was ranked by percentage revenue growth during the period 2020 to 2023. To qualify, companies must have been founded and generating revenue by March 31, 2020. They had to be U.S.-based, privately held, for-profit, and independent—not subsidiaries or divisions of other companies—as of December 31, 2023. The 2023 Inc. 5000 was ranked by percentage revenue growth during the period 2019 to 2022. To qualify, companies must have been founded and generating revenue by March 31, 2019. They had to be U.S.-based, privately held, for-profit, and independent—not subsidiaries or divisions of other companies—as of December 31, 2022. The 2022 Inc. 5000 was ranked by percentage revenue growth during the period 2018 to 2021. To qualify, companies must have been founded and generating revenue by March 31, 2018. They had to be U.S.-based, privately held, for-profit, and independent—not subsidiaries or divisions of other companies—as of December 31, 2021. The 2021 Inc. 5000 was ranked by percentage revenue growth during the period 2017 to 2020. To qualify, companies must have been founded and generating revenue by March 31, 2017. They had to be U.S.-based, privately held, for-profit, and independent—not subsidiaries or divisions of other companies—as of December 31, 2020. The 2020 Inc. 5000 was ranked by percentage revenue growth during the period 2016 to 2019. To qualify, companies must have been founded and generating revenue by

March 31, 2016. They had to be U.S.-based, privately held, for-profit, and independent—not subsidiaries or divisions of other companies—as of December 31, 2019. The 2017 Inc. 5000 was ranked by percentage revenue growth during the period 2013 to 2016. To qualify, companies must have been founded and generating revenue by March 31, 2013. They had to be U.S.-based, privately held, for-profit, and independent—not subsidiaries or divisions of other companies—as of December 31, 2016.

McAdam furnished Inc. Magazine with financial information for award evaluation but did not make or receive any payment in association with the award. Several companies presented on this list have gone public or have been acquired. The minimum revenue required for 2020 was $100,000; the minimum for 2023 was $2 million. Inc. reserves the right to decline applicants for subjective reasons. Companies on the Inc. 5000 list were featured by Inc. They represent the top tier of the Inc. 5000, which can be found at www.inc.com/inc5000.

*USA Today Best Financial Advisory Firms*
This award was granted by USA Today, with assistance from Statista, in 2023 & 2024. McAdam LLC did not apply for or pay for the award. For the full methodology of the award, please visit: https://r.statista.com/en/licensing/americas-best-financial-advisory-firms-2024/award/.

*AdvisoryHQ's Top Rated Wealth Management Firms*
AdvisoryHQ News Corp is a California-based editorial, research, and ranking company that operates in the U.S., Canada, U.K., and Australia. AdvisoryHQ is owned by Market Consensus, a Nevada corporation. Each year, AdvisoryHQ conducts due diligence to identify, select, and rank companies in various industries, including financial services, wealth management, investment management, and financial advisory, amongst others. AdvisoryHQ reviews and ranking articles are independently researched and objectively written. In order to be included in any AdvisoryHQ ranking list, firms have to pass AdvisoryHQ's selective methodologies. Firms such as McAdam do not pay for their ranking.

In assessing its pool of candidates for top financial advisors, AdvisoryHQ uses a multi-step selection methodology for identifying, researching, and generating its ranking list. AdvisoryHQ's Top-Down Advisor Selection Methodology methodologies are based on a wide range of filters, including: quality of services provided, overall value provided, transparency, customized services, history of innovation, customer experience (positive and negative), level of independence, team excellence, and other criteria. Below is a step-by-step overview of AdvisoryHQ's methodology process. AdvisoryHQ reviews and ranks advisory companies only; it does not rank individual financial professionals.

Step 1: Using publicly available sources, AdvisoryHQ identifies a wide range of firms that are providing services in a designated area (city, state, or local geographic location).

Step 2: AdvisoryHQ's review team then applies initial methodology filters to narrow down the list of identified firms/products. These filters include company strengths, trustworthiness, transparency, professional reputation, managed assets, ROI/ROA effectiveness, fee structure, what customers/clients are saying about the organization, and other criteria.

Step 3: After reducing the initial list, AdvisoryHQ then assesses the remaining firms. The award criteria take into account a range of factors, including experience level, level of customization, site quality, resources, features, range of provided services, innovation, value-added, and many more factors, to build up a broad picture of what each firm or product has to offer before the final selection process occurs.

Step 4: Based on the results of performed assessment, AdvisoryHQ's research and selection team then finalizes the list of entities that make it into its top rated publications, which are then published to the general public. Candidates are ranked on a scale from one (1) to five (5). Recipients are then listed with their corresponding ratings and highlighted features.

With respect to AdvisoryHQ's "Top Financial Advisors in Philadelphia, Pennsylvania," McAdam LLC received the ranking in 2020. In 2019, 9 Financial Advisors received recognition for the ranking.

Made in the USA
Middletown, DE
26 February 2025

71867882R00096